CATTLE BOAT TO OXFORD

The Education of R. I. W. Westgate

Edited from His Letters, Diaries & Papers

SHEILA MARGARET WESTGATE

Introduction by
LOUIS AUCHINCLOSS

Walker and Company

New York

First published in the United States of America in 1994
by Walker Publishing Company, Inc.

Published simultaneously in Canada
by Thomas Allen & Son Canada, Ltd.,
Markham, Ontario, Canada

Library of Congress Cataloging-in-Publication Data
Westgate, R. I. W. (Reginald Isaac Wilfred), 1904–1988
    Cattle boat to Oxford : the education of R. I. W. Westgate : edited
from his letters, diaries & papers / Sheila Margaret Westgate :
introduction by Louis Auchincloss.
        p.   cm.
    Includes index.
    ISBN 0–8027–1300–9
    1. Westgate, R. I. W. (Reginald Isaac Wilfred), 1904–1988.
2. Teachers—United States—Biography. 3. University of Oxford—
Students—Diaries. I. Westgate, Sheila M. Dann. II. Title
LA2317.W39A3 1994
370' .92—dc20   94–13580
[B]   CIP

PRINTED IN THE U.S.A
2 4 6 8 10 9 7 5 3 1

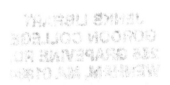

For
Bill's children
and
grandchildren

CONTENTS

Foreword   ix

Introduction   xi

I   *"The Harvest In Africa"*   1
(1904—1907)

II   *"Wayfarers From Belfast"*   5
(1907—1920)

III   *"Two Memorable Summer Jobs"*   16
(1920—1922)

IV   *"Feed Them Bleeding Cattle!"*   34
(May—June, 1923)

V   *"I've Come To See the Master of Balliol"*   44
(June—July, 1923)

VI   *"Could You Say When I Sail?"*   54
(August, 1923)

VII   *"You May Gather That I Am Confused"*   63
(July—November, 1924)

VIII   *"Songs & Howls & Pokers On Pails"*   77
(November, 1924—March, 1925)

IX   *"I Hoped To Be a Great Headmaster"*   98
(June—August, 1925)

X   *"At Last I Am At Oxford"*   110
(October—December, 1925)

XI   *"A Very Pleasant Pupil"*   123
(January—July, 1926)

XII   *"I Am Phenomenally Lucky"*   135
(July—October, 1926)

XIII   *"Mingling With Humanity Is A Noble Thing"*   149
(November, 1926—January, 1927)

XIV   *"Tomorrow To Fresh Fields"*   161
(March—April, 1927)

XV   *Down the Staircase & Up With School*   180

XVI   *Reflections By His Children*   187

Index   192

FOREWORD

THESE ARE THE LETTERS that Bill wrote to his family from 1921 to 1927, which we found in Bristol, England, after his sister Maureen's death. The letters are augmented by passages from the autobiographical manuscript he started shortly before his death, indicated in the book by the heading AUTOBIOGRAPHY. In 1968 he wrote an article for the Brooks School alumni magazine in which he refers to his later years, reprinted as Chapter XV of this book. I have tried to fill other gaps in his story where I had the knowledge to do so, and have designated these passages by SMW. Basically, this book is a revelation of Bill's formative years. His English spellings and vernacular have been preserved.

I could not have accomplished this work without the help of many people. First I would like to mention the late Sam Walker of Walker Publishing Company who offered me his help. I am sorry he cannot see the fruition carried on by his family. Next came Bowden Broadwater who spent an entire week reading letters covering Bill's whole life. It was he who pointed out the unique quality of Bill's early writings and suggested the title *Cattleboat to Oxford*.

My next great helper was Ann Dewey with whom I had great fun cutting out extraneous material from the letters and organizing them for publication. Then came Beth Walker and her son Ramsey, the new head of Walker and Company, who took up the project where Sam had left off. They provided me with a most congenial editor, Jack Hinshaw, who transcribed and typeset the hand-written letters. My family has been most helpful with proofreading. Last, but far from least, I thank Louis Auchincloss for his sensitive and warm introduction.

—Sheila Margaret Westgate
Chatham, Massachusetts
October, 1993

INTRODUCTION

ANY WELL TOLD STORY of the struggles of a sensitive and deeply thinking man in educating himself to be of some use to a world of multiple contradictions, whether it be those of a privileged scion of statesmen like Henry Adams or of the Welsh miner in *The Corn Is Green*, is sure to grip our attention, and Bill Westgate's tale is no exception. What is such a story but a microcosm of the process of civilization itself? His letters as a student in Canada and England, amplified by excerpts from an unfinished autobiography, vividly recreate the great headmaster that his more fortunate readers will remember: wise, witty and brave, touchingly humane and humble, though never at the cost of a sturdy self-respect.

The process of education was not an easy one for him. He had the assets of a loving and caring family in Winnipeg, good health and athletic ability, but the Westgate means were exiguous, and Bill's boyhood dream of Oxford seemed destined to remain only that. He had to work in summers as a surveyor's assistant and as a teacher of non-English speaking Indian children in the wilderness. He suffered from religious doubts, tormenting to the son of a deeply devout cleric who had once been a heroic missionary in Africa. And for all his long and faithful adherence to classical studies, he had moments of cruel disillusionment at Trinity College in Toronto when he feared that he might be "congenitally incapable of discerning any intelligent purpose in half the lines of Virgil." But worst of all, when he had worked his way to England to apply for a scholarship supposedly available to sons of ministers, risking serious injury on the lower deck of a cattle boat while roping Texas longhorns, suspended in the air above their eponymous projections, it was only to find that the opening was for sons of <u>resident</u> clergymen.

In the end, however, like a god from the machine in the Greek dramas he so loved, the Rhodes scholarship was won, and he found himself enrolled in Balliol College. "At length and at last," he wrote exultantly to his father on November 4, 1925, "I am at Oxford." Joy brought out the poet in him:

> I could find it in me to shift to another time some description of the quiet beauty of it all; but the wide gravel walk between two dewy lawns is now half-covered with ruddy brown leaves that fell overnight from the two massive chestnuts that stand sentinel by my study window. At every gentle gust these two great beings rustle as though whispering their hurried goodbye to the hundred withering leaves that straightway break their stems and flutter, flutter, flutter to the ground.

Financial worries were now largely over, and Bill entertained his family with vivid and sometimes very funny accounts of college revels and personalities, boat racing, beagling, house parties (he even met Lady Astor and the Prince of Wales) and wonderful bicycle tours over England. He may have had too many extra-curricular activities, and he was sadly downhearted when he had to inform his father that he had attained only a third class in Honor Moderations ("Mods"), but those who knew him as a headmaster would never regret the wider education that he attained and so richly enjoyed in the England of those years. And, of course, in the end he did receive his Oxford degree in Classics, and went on to his great career at Harvard, Radcliffe, Andover, Brooks and Saint Bernard's.

—Louis Auchincloss
October, 1993

— I —
"THE HARVEST IN AFRICA"
(1904—1907)

SMW

Reginald Isaac Wilfred Westgate, known in early years as "Wilfred" and later by his own choice called "Bill," was born on September 14, 1904 in the Kiboriani Hills in the district of Mpwapwa, German East Africa. His father, Thomas Buchanan Reginald Westgate (called "Rex") was born in Watford, Ontario, Canada, of Protestant farming parents whose ancestors had migrated from Ireland in the nineteenth century.

Rex taught school for a few years, but became inspired to do missionary work and attended Huron Theological College, later part of the University of Western Ontario. He was first sent to Paraguay, but after a couple of years realized that the natives could not be reached satisfactorily until they became less migratory. He and his fellow missionary, Edmund Crawford, asked the Church Missionary Society (CMS) of London to transfer them to other fields. They were both sent to Africa; Crawford to British East Africa (now Kenya) and Rex to German East Africa (now Tanzania) where there had been a British mission before Germany had been granted that part of Africa by the Treaty of Berlin in 1890.

In Mombasa the friends met and later married two sisters, Henrietta and Kathleen Malone. Wilfred's mother, Henrietta Georgina Humphrey Malone (called "Rita") was the daughter of a cultivated Irish family, whose antecedents included Anthony Malone (1700-1776), Chancellor of the Exchequer and eloquent orator of the Irish parliament, and his nephew, Edmund Malone (1741-1812), the Shakespearean scholar.

The early death of the parents of the Malone girls left them without home ties, and Kathleen in 1898 and Rita in 1901 proceeded to East Africa as missionaries. Rex arrived in Mombasa in 1902 and shortly met Rita at the Bishop's house. After he had passed the required examination in Swahili and recovered from being shot while boar hunting, they were married on October 13, 1903.

Despite fever, they survived the march of two hundred miles on foot or in a hammock to their destination in the Kiboriani Hills. Here Rex was to build a sanatorium for missionaries, but until this was accomplished their shelter was a tent. One room was ready by the time Wilfred was born, but a few days later the thatched roof caught fire and mother and baby were carried out to a tent. As the source of water was at some distance and buckets had to be carried by hand, the building was gutted and it was a month before the building could be used again. On November 27th a bad fire came near their settlement and there was great difficulty beating it out.

There was much illness among the natives and Rita, a trained nurse, ran a clinic for them. In December Wilfred became ill with measles and the cook's child, who had been baptized with him, died of the disease.

A daughter, Maureen (later called "Moll") was born on October 25, 1905. At this time there was a serious revolt among the tribesmen against the Germans; all the missionaries from a large area came to stay at Kiboriani and a troop of German soldiers was sent to guard them. Much rain and heavy gales delayed the completion of the sanatorium.

In 1906 Rex wrote to his brother Palmer that it was difficult to do missionary work in the tropics with two children to look after; that they were due to go home on leave the next year; and that he hoped to make some arrangements for the children to stay in England.

Meanwhile Wilfred and Maureen were tended by native girls and spoke only the Chigogo language. Rita took control of the dispensary and school work while Rex continued with the building of the sanatorium and church, as well as his religious duties, which often involved treks to far away settlements. He also made visits to the government center of Tabora and hunting trips for their only meat.

Reports to headquarters in London also had to be made. In one of these he wrote "Truly the harvest in Africa is great and difficult to gather, but it will repay the labor. No converts in any other land seem so capable of the highest forms of the peculiarly Christian life as do those of Africa. Facility of forgiveness, simplicity, affection, aptitude to rest on a Higher Power, and lowly docility of heart are some of these. A people born of ages of oppression and sin, yet capable of these, are worth striving for."

On August 27, 1907 the Westgate family of four with many porters left Kiboriani for the long journey to England. Three weeks were allowed for the safari on foot to the coast. A native boy, Samweli, accompanied them to England to help look after the children. After 54 days, they reached Dover and were welcomed by Mrs. Armitage, a benefactor of missionaries, to her home in Hampstead.

A few months later Rex was sent on deputation work to Canada for seven months, where he raised money and showed slides for his mission in Africa. Rita and the children went to Portrush in Ireland to be near a sister and her children. On Rex's return to England the family moved to rooms in Redhill, Surrey, to be near their cousins, the Price family. Rita's third child, Dorothy, was born here on June 10th, 1909.

Rex, meanwhile, was due back in Africa and sailed from England on October 7, 1908, this time for Bugiri, German East Africa. Rita and Dorothy left in September, 1909 to rejoin Rex at his new station, where they stayed for four years. Before she departed, Rita had made satisfactory arrangements for the two older children to remain in England. This was a common practice in those days when many Englishmen lived overseas where the climate and conditions were not suitable for the education and health of the children. Rita later wrote:

> I left them in the very loving and efficient care of the Rev. and Mrs. Nightingale and their large family [of seven girls and one boy of Wilfred's age], and of Miss Coe, who had been governess in the family for some years. It was a lovely old place with large grounds and gardens, and the squire and landlord of the estate was Sir John Kennaway, the loved and honored president of the Church Missionary Society. It was an ideal home for children, and as they and others played in the garden it has been likened to a "children's paradise." Shortly after leaving Wilfred and Maureen there, I set sail for Africa with Dorothy, aged four months.

So successful was her choice that on the parent's return to claim their children Maureen declared "I don't want to be a Westgate. I want to be a Nightingale."

— II —
"WAYFARERS FROM BELFAST"
(1907—1920)

AUTOBIOGRAPHY

There was Mr Nightingale, who took daily prayers in the big dining room when all the household—maids, cooks, gardeners, dairymaid, groom, the large Nightingale family and we infants—all met for a Bible reading, a hymn, prayers when we knelt at our chairs, and a blessing....This was soon followed by lessons in letters and figures, reading and writing, stories and geography, singing and piano, even dancing and manners...We had breaks, of course, indoors or out, and a jungle gym on the lawn with a rope and ladder...A third boy, Joe Allen, joined our schoolroom contingent for about three years; the ages of the boys were all within about three weeks of each other.

The arrival of Brownie the pony enlarged our young lives, for we could ride him in the meadow almost at any time. When grown-up hunters had "meets" throughout the winter to hunt foxes past the Big Woods and past the Church Meadows, we boys could take it in turns to polish up Brownie, attend the meeting of towering hunters at Fairmile Corner, a quarter of a mile away, and follow the hunt amid forty giant horses. We were soon outridden in the open field and often in the excitement fell off Brownie, but remounted and rode him home to resume lessons as usual in the schoolroom.

Now and again we visited the sea at Sidmouth, Devon. Once or twice we visited Exeter Museum (I remember a whale's jaw there), and once we saw the Honiton Horse Show. At Christmas there were parties at the great Escot House [home of Sir John Kennaway] with children's dances, Punch and Judy shows and musical chairs. Once I drove eight miles away, an unheard of exploration, with Tom the Gardener and Tom the Horse to fetch live turkeys. There was also a Nightingale wedding at which Ted and I were pages dressed in silk shirts, black velvet suits and patent leather shoes. The vicarage was gorgeously decorated. Maureen also was beautifully dressed up, but too shy to take any part at all.

Such were the four blissful years that Mother had steered us to in Edwardian Devon. It was rich in all that children could want; health, learning, habits, principles, manners, simple goodness and piety, poetry, laughter, discipline, plain teaching most carefully observed and maintained every day, and ample scope for free wonder and enjoyment.

Our Edwardian country life with "Toe" [Miss Coe] and all the Escot household ended just before Christmas, 1912, when our parents came down and took us by train to Croydon. Here we began life in a rather poky semi-detached house with a small, overlooked garden at 33 Moreland Avenue. Luckily our Crawford cousins, issues of a marriage in Mombasa in 1903, had a house diagonally across from us, and we cautiously began to make friends with them and run across to each other's house and garden. Almost all other features of our new life we found different, horrible, woeful! No companionable maids and servants, no pony stable, no St. Bernard dog "Lion," no farmyard cats and chickens, no spacious gardens and nearby meadows.

Moreland Avenue was a decent street, but one was expected to walk on the sidewalk; this I remember outraged my sense of freedom. On the other hand, I liked the many shops, the roaring busses that whisked you downtown, the traffic, mostly horse-drawn, the perilous crossings, the vibrant ring of city life, the animated snatches of Cockney talk. I don't remember Christmas Day particularly, or New Year's, for we had no friends yet but Aunt Kathleen and Uncle Eddie Crawford and Bea (8), Emily (7) and Walter (4) on nearby St. Vincent's Road, and they had barely settled in themselves.

The chief attraction for me was little Dorothy, my newly found sister (4) fresh from Africa. Neither had seen such a sibling and we played together on the floor or sofa a great deal, rather to Maureen's neglect. We had an oldish cockney maid, Kate, pious and God-fearing, yet fun-loving, who would play much with the cat and chatter with us and Mother. Father I think went often to the CMS office near St. Paul's in London to confer with the all-important Secretary, Mr Manley. I believe Mr Manley had a high opinion of my father's work and devotion to duty around Mpwapwa, East Africa.

SMW

In October, 1913 Rex returned to Africa, supposedly for a year, after which the family were to settle in Canada, where they could all be together. He had been offered the position of Field Secretary of the Anglican Church Missionary Society of Canada.

Meanwhile Rita and the children would stay in Croydon where she could be near her sister. Schools were found for the two older children. Wilfred fitfully attended the Whitgift Grammar School, an institution of high scholastic standing. He found the other boys rough and alien after his sheltered life in Devon, and later owned that he frequently feigned illness to escape attendance.

AUTOBIOGRAPHY

Much more vivid was Mother's plan to visit Ireland in August, 1914 where we would stay in real country rectories, see real country cousins called Malone and Watson. Though grownup or at Trinity College, Dublin, they would be exciting. There would be a tennis court and a big house and drives and country roads to walk with no sidewalks curbing one's freedom! A gathering cloud, however, began immediately to shadow this vision. The assassination at Sarajevo in July of the Archduke Ferdinand began to stir rumors of spreading war that might pit the ambitious German army and navy against Britain. How, my Mother must have worried, would this affect Father's life in German East Africa, his planned return to England and our subsequent emigration to Canada? I, aged nearly ten, felt some of her anxiety and began to scan our newspaper, the *Daily*

Express. We were to cross to Ireland on August 6th and war was declared on Germany August 4th. Maureen had delightedly been sent off to Escot for the short holiday, but Mother, Dorothy and I made our way towards Ireland by train, crowded now with Irish troops moving to or from Liverpool, noisy and unruly. At the dockside we took the magic evening steamer that brought us into Belfast harbor on a sunlit morning, August 7th. We were soon on the train for Moy, County Tyrone and there were met by the tall and bearded Uncle John Watson and Aunt Beatrice who drove us three to their rectory, a place of bliss to my happy eyes. We were to have spent a week there, another week with Uncle Albert Malone ten miles away and then go home to Croydon. Alas, how differently Fate and the country doctor arranged things for us!

At the Watsons' was a jolly cousin Kathleen (16), soon to go to Trinity, Dublin like her brothers, and a more serious cousin Cyril, shortly to emigrate to Canada to seek his fortune. Kathleen took me to buy stout country boots, and promised to take me mushrooming at six on Monday morning, so I sat happily at supper on Sunday night. I felt a "stitch" in my side, however, and when it persisted Mother sent me upstairs. Halfway up it grew worse, so I was put to bed and an irregular pulse was felt. It's a not uncommon feature in children, but amid all her other anxieties Mother's mind was filled with fears and Dr Fergus was sent for. The irregular pulse impressed him and he prescribed total rest in bed for the indefinite future! Immediately gone were the 6 o'clock hunt for mushrooms and the visit next week to Uncle Albert and Aunt Arabella Malone at Benburb near Armagh. I felt sorry for myself under this mistaken diagnosis during the long months of August to March, though it was an insidious privilege to be attended and cosseted by a concerned Mother and faithful younger Dorothy who answered my calls and brought me books and games. My uncles and aunts cheered me up, but the cousins in both houses went off in September to school or college and appeared not until Christmas.

While Maureen led her familiar happy life in Escot in a large household still not much shaken in its country ways by the war, we led a most restricted and closeted, if privileged, life. It was saintly of the Watsons and Malones to house and feed and nurse us. Social life there was none that I remember. Mother and Dorothy took walks; I was supplied with books and first began to read and reread Ballantine and Henty and *The Illustrated London News*. Life was totally uneventful and I, or we, had no contact with our peers. To this extent my life was unhealthily withdrawn and self-centered, making me shy and self-absorbed for all my youthful years.

It ended abruptly, for Mother took me in March to specialists in Belfast who recommended that we return to our rented house in Croydon and also see a famous heart specialist, Sir James McKenzie. His examination led to a curt opinion that there was nothing at all seriously wrong with me; that the irregularity of heartbeat had no significance in a healthy boy; I should go back to school and play football. I was shocked to think how ordinary I was and how two terms of school had been so oddly spent in bed in Ireland, but resumed my life at Whitgift as best I could after such an absence.

Meanwhile, like all England but unlike Ireland, wartime Croydon was suffering shortages of food and fuel. Rents also would be lower in Ireland and Mother's brother and sister, Uncle Albert and Aunt Beatrice, advised her to move out of Croydon to Belfast where they could do more to watch and help her. They had already, God knows, done much!

Zeppelins began to fly over London that winter and dropped three bombs in a triangular pattern round our house, shattering our sleep one midnight and leaving a gaping hole at the corner of Moreland Avenue where I passed daily. I stopped to see the torn fences and broken windows and the yawning crater where once had been our doctor's tennis court, and at school I heard of other damaged sites. School continued but Mother accelerated her plans by packing to move on December 14th, 1915 to Belfast, where we would occupy rented furnished rooms for a while, and the children be put to school.

The Church Missionary Society must have continued to pay
Father's salary to Mother during his internment in Africa, but
we were hard up those months of moving and packing and deep
uncertainty. Mother's fortitude and good nature around the age
of fifty were themselves a miracle, though taken as a matter of
course by us children of eleven, ten and seven. A genial middle-
aged cousin, Alfred Malone, helped Mother find rooms, which
proved far too small, and later a house for rent on the edge of
Belfast; he must also have helped Mother find a girls' school,
Miss Rentoul's, for Maureen and Dorothy, and a fine sturdy
boys' school for me, where I began shyly on January 17, 1916.
This was the Royal Belfast Academical Institute, founded about
1820. It was rough and "common" compared with the polite
Whitgift, but instruction was mostly thorough and interesting,
especially to me who had been out of school for nearly a year.
This caused a certain shyness itself, and so did being a new boy
entering late in the year; still more of a difficulty was trying to
assimilate my accent to the Irish voices around me. Happily no
great fun was made of my different accent and I fell into the
Belfast patterns of speech.

In my second year I was befriended by a fierce-appearing
bachelor master of perhaps fifty who taught mostly advanced
Latin up in the Sixth Form [12th grade] and coached their rugby
football, but also taught some younger boys. "Mr Gee," as we
called him, persuaded me to begin Greek at the age of twelve. In
a small class of four I enjoyed the excitement of a new alphabet,
a new view of the New Testament written in the language that
God had chosen for his revelation of the Gospel; and I also found
Xenophon's story of the March of the Ten Thousand through
Asia Minor easy and exciting. To Mr Gee's lively, sometimes
irascible, Greek teaching I owe a lifelong interest in Greek
literature and what success I had later in teaching Greek at the
University of Western Ontario, Harvard and Radcliffe, Andover,
Brooks and occasionally at St. Bernard's school in New York
City.

Mr Gee must have been wretchedly underpaid, though he
was a graduate of Oxford, for he bicycled to school from the

suburbs in all weathers, and when an accident tore one trouser leg badly he mended it with only a large safety pin which he used for a week or two; in the rough atmosphere of the "Institute" such eccentricities mattered little. Despite such poverty, Mr Gee regularly invited half a dozen boys to his house every Saturday afternoon to play tennis on nearby courts, or for pingpong in his overcrowded sitting-dining room, or for bridge and stories and other games. Such dedication to his students filled his days, and in the summer he organized short bicycle trips round County Antrim. No wonder we were fond of him and worked very hard and successfully in his fierce classes. In these fatherless years, aged eleven, twelve and thirteen (1915-1918), while Father was lost to view in German East Africa, school was much enhanced when I came somehow into Mr Gee's friendly circle. I gladly bicycled five miles across Belfast to join him on Saturdays, and it must have relieved Mother to have me thus engaged.

Occasionally we had the delight of a country week or two for school holidays in County Tyrone or County Armagh. I also was sent down alone to Aunt Beatrice and Uncle John to recover from some childish sickness, and found myself revelling in the once-familiar solitude of their rectory. By lamplight in a large rectory bedroom I felt a thrill in reading the denunciations and prophecies of Isaiah while the windows rattled in the wintry air. We all belonged to the Scripture Union and read religiously the daily appointed passages of the Bible.

As World War I turned in favor of the Allies, missionaries escaping from German East Africa reached England and Ireland. A Miss Forsythe, who came to live with us, had seen Father in internment. On release by the Belgian forces from the Congo, Father had joined the British army in 1916 as an interpreter and chaplain, and was made a Captain. He was invalided out in 1917 and was destined to spend some time in a British hospital in Cairo, and then five difficult months in the Royal Victoria Hospital in Belfast. His homecoming to the family was dramatic. Mother went to meet him in London and encountered a bombing of the Strand Palace Hotel, while I was in charge of the family at 30 Cardigan Drive, Belfast. I went to meet my parents at the Belfast station, and was immensely proud of my burly, sun-tanned father in Captain's uniform. I little knew how ill his experiences had left him. We fitted happily into our small house, no longer without a father or captain. We all took walks together, Father preached in churches and I helped him open long-packed books. We had some vacation again at Aunt Beatrice's in August, and in November Father went into a long and dangerous period in hospital, where I was occasionally allowed to visit him after school.

SMW

Rex was operated on for gall stones and his gall bladder was removed. The following January one lung was removed. He had frequent bouts of fever, dysentery and pneumonia. His poor condition was considered to be a result of his internment in East Africa by the Germans.

AUTOBIOGRAPHY

Father's long illness dragged heavily, with Mother in constant attendance in times of crisis. No plans for our destined migration to Canada could be made till his health was assured. His slow convalescence ended in April, 1918 after five months as a patient. Again in August we enjoyed County Tyrone for a month. Then, having given up our rented house, we moved into an elegant borrowed one with electric light and telephone for September while we negotiated for a passage across the stormy Atlantic. This eventually took place a week after the explosive excitement of Armistice Day, November 11, 1918. Whistles blew, bells rang and sirens sounded at 11 o'clock that morning as we were all out for a secluded walk on the banks of the Lagan in cool sunshine, Father still using a cane.

We children did not attend school that fall term, so time hung heavy on our hands while passages were being arranged and then postponed until the war should end. At last the night came for crossing to Liverpool in the darkness, and at dawn on November 20th we transferred to the wretchedly small ship

Metagama bound for St John's, New Brunswick. Father and I had one cabin with a brawny Scot who had been torpedoed once and let us know of it; Mother, Maureen and Dorothy had another. I remember agonies of seasickness and stormy seas when I ventured more dead than alive on deck; Dorothy at ten proved the heartiest sailor.

No improvement occurred in the weather before we entered the Bay of Fundy and tied up at 11 a.m. on November 30th, towering above the dock at high tide in St. John's. The scenery was dreary, but it was good to scamper ashore and explore the dockland. We were sorry not to see the famous Reversible [sic] Falls, but of course by evening when we returned to the *Metagama* she was far below the morning's level at the dockside, so we had that demonstration of the Bay of Funday's unique tidal movement.

After dark we climbed aboard a luxurious Pullman, were fed a gargantuan supper and then rolled comfortably into well-made beds and sped through New Brunswick and Maine till morning light revealed the wintry landscape and bitter chill of the Provinces of Quebec and eastern Ontario. I remember no towns or stops or landings, all of which could have been interesting. At last, in the evening of December 2nd, we rolled into the station at Toronto and a childless couple called Williams most kindly welcomed all five of us wayfarers from Belfast into their most hospitable and comfortable city home. They were not used to children or a family invasion, but fed and entertained us handsomely for about two weeks. There was snow on the ground and University of Toronto School boys had cheerful skirmishes outside, but I was a stranger dressed in Belfast shorts and jersey, and we got to know no children. Father was busy at headquarters of the Missionary Society of the Canadian Church (MSCC), especially with Canon Gould, its vigorous secretary, and had at last, three years after accepting his position as Field Secretary in 1914, begun to prepare to assume his duties. It was indeed saintly of the Williams couple to accept us for so long.

About December 6th Father and I left for his boyhood home, Watford [about twenty miles west of London, Ontario]. His father had died during the war, but his mother, aged and bowed, lived in the old homestead with her youngest son Alec and several of his children, including my cousins Ralph and Alma.

The three hour wintry train ride was thrilling, and more so to find Uncle Alec at Watford station in deep snow with a horse and cutter to whisk us over a snowy road five miles to the hospitable if rough and ready homestead. After the isolation of Toronto, I loved finding the company of warm-hearted new uncles and aunts and their numerous if shy and wondering children, for Uncle Will had another homestead nearby on RR 4. I had never seen food like cream served so plentifully or with so little heed to style, but with such noisy pleasure. Outdoors next day I found work horses and a huge hay barn where we could play by the hour, and fields stretching far out to where the railway cut across them a mile away. Bedding and toilet arrangements were primitive but snug and I took to my new relatives. Father relaxed and was the center of attention as the farm boy wonder and wartime hero in the little community.

Three days later Mother brought Maureen and Dorothy on from Toronto and we all fitted in rather crowdedly. It was disappointing to her to find life so primitive and stark, so we all moved on in a few days for Christmas with Father's favorite brother, the Reverend Palmer Westgate and his wife, our Aunt Minnie, going by train to Sandwich and their rectory of St John's Church. This was a most congenial house not unlike Aunt Beatrice's in County Tyrone. Here we spent a happy week, including Christmas and New Year, enjoying two small boys aged two and three who sadly were both to die in childhood. A later sister, Margaret, survived and became one of my favorite cousins. A brother, Alan Westgate, became my godson but also died in childhood at about fourteen years of age. Our sojourn with the Palmer Westgates gave us a quiet interlude, very welcome to Mother who found Minnie wholly congenial—her first friend in Canada!

From these three stopping places, Toronto, Watford and Sandwich, we then went to Hamilton, Ontario to a commodious modern house lent for six months while Father decided on a place to live as Field Secretary of the CCMS. Again we were put to school, which we had not seen since last July! My school, called Highfield, was very small, perhaps forty boys, and understaffed by an elderly Cambridge headmaster and one or two assistants. The Head held three classes in one room at three long tables forming a hollow square. Classes might be doing Latin and math and English all at one time, commanding the Head's attention in succession. He completed this with a switch that brought wanderers up sharp. Strange to say, we learned something from each other in this disorganized scene, which perhaps owed something to wartime conditions.

I stayed in Hamilton only from January to July, but learned to skate there and enjoyed bicycle rides in its handsome countryside. I had my first sailing with friendly school companions, and also my first severe sunburn pedalling home from Burlington Beach. The schooling was disappointing and I secretly worked ahead in my Belfast *Euclid* as far as I could. There was, however, no Greek and wretched Latin.

— III —
"TWO MEMORABLE SUMMER JOBS"
(1920—1922)

AUTOBIOGRAPHY

Father had decided on Winnipeg, Manitoba for our home. We set
out to go there by train to Fort McNicoll, then by boat to Fort
William over Lakes Huron and Superior, and finally by train the
remaining three hundred miles. First, however, we had the
privilege of a glorious day at Niagara Falls so that we might see
the greatest sight in the East before settling in the prairies.
Considering family income and expenses, Niagara was a handsome gesture, vividly remembered.

Sailing across the Great Lakes is most comfortable. The
large ferries connect with trains that carry you to Winnipeg and
beyond. In Winnipeg we stayed with a hospitable Dr Knipe at
Deer Lodge, and after some house hunting, found 513 McMillan
Avenue on the southern outskirts.

I was quickly enrolled at St John's College School[1] in the far
north end [of Winnipeg] and provided with a bicycle to get there
as a day boy. The school was easy on a shy, new boy and provided me with some excellent teachers; especially in my third
year with a splendid Oxford teacher of Latin and Greek with
whom I studied tutorially for a whole year in Homer and Plato.
He was a victim of the Great War, suffering in Silesian coal
mines, finding no employment in the 1920s, drifting to western
Canada where our headmaster, Mr Walter Burman, astutely
added him to the school staff. He became alcoholic, stayed with
us for some weeks (in a totally unalcoholic family that never
could afford a drink had they wanted one!), left our house and
became lost to view.

Another splendid teacher was the young Canon William de Pauley, a Dublin Gold Medalist, who taught philosophy and theology for a few years in St John's College. Nothing else was brilliant except our St John's hockey. We had a covered rink, long before artificial ice appeared, and all ages could use it at appropriate hours from early October to mid-April; its mere cover guaranteed perpetual shade and cold. Its most prominent graduates in my day were my classmate, Murray Murdock, later a brilliant member of the New York Rangers and later still head hockey coach of Yale and director of Yale's athletics; and his cousin, Andy Blair, who played for the Toronto Maple Leafs. An elderly and lame English master, who could not skate, gave the youngest boys, the Midgets, excellent instruction. Endless hours of skating and playing in a very cold rink seemed to do the rest.

While in college I had two memorable summer jobs. When I was sixteen and starting to work on a farm near Winnipeg, Father telephoned from Dauphin [about 200 miles northwest of Winnipeg] to say that a job as a surveyor's boy was available at $90 per month, and advised me to take the night train to Dauphin. I arrived on Sunday morning and went to church with him and then to Judge and Mrs Bonnycastle and their jolly family of four boys and two girls.

A stream flowed through their few acres and the Judge had built a clay tennis court. How many hours I spent on Sundays or after work on weekdays in their company on that enchanted ground, much like a Canadian Escot where I was welcome all summer. A swimming hole was nearby. I revered the shrewd and witty Judge and gladly mowed his lawn for him to practice putting. I gradually fell in love with both his wife, a lady of breeding who settled in the Red River Valley near Winnipeg, and their elder daughter "Gussie" (for Augusta), so the summer passed quickly.

My work was to drive out at 7 a.m. every fine day in a battered T-model farm car with an English veteran, Harold Crowe and lay out roads, ditches and culverts with careful surveyor's measurements and numerous pegs set in place. I held a surveyor's pole and Harold took readings. Then we both hammered in pegs. Days later came teams of men and horses with large scoops to model new ditches and road surfaces, chop trees if need be, and in the blazing sun create passable roadways through the brush. I loved the rather solitary work with Jim and we had very little to do with the rough contractors, axemen and diggers who executed our plans. By 5 p.m. we would usually be back in Dauphin for a shower and then an evening of tennis before I went back to my quiet lodging with farmer and Mrs O'Neill.

[1] Saint John's College School (now St John's-Ravenscourt) and Saint John's College were both affiliated with the University of Manitoba. Bill took his first year in Arts at the school and then transferred for the last three to the college. He graduated from the University in May, 1924, and enrolled for the next year at Trinity College, Toronto as a graduate student in classics to prepare for Oxford.

LETTERS

The Rectory, Dauphin
Sunday Night, [May 15, 1921]

My Dear Mother,

I arrived safely here about 9 $^{o'c}$ this morning & had breakfast with Mr Barrett. After church I went to the Bonnycastles & stayed there till 9^{30} this evening. They have a pretty big cottage with tennis court, any amount of ground & a stream running through it. The youngsters sail about it on a raft.

I am to go to the Municipal Hall tomorrow morning at 8 in my working clothes & with lunch, & I suppose I shall be out on the road till 7 at night. I don't think we shall ever be out of Dauphin for the night all summer, so I shall have to arrange for board and lodging here. Mr B. says he doesn't know how much I am to get!

Please excuse this scribble, as it is just midnight, & I have to be up pretty early.

Love to all, Bill

Dauphin
July 10th, 1921

Dear Moll [Bill's sister]

Last Thursday, Harold Crowe & I drove off to Sifton, about 22 miles away, in a hired car,—Poor Lizzie is now being internally inspected by a garage man. Sifton is a Galician settlement, & few people there can speak understandable English. The councillor of Sifton, however, met us & after waiting an hour on the roadside, he brought us a wagon to finish our journey. The wagon already contained two Galician women with babies in arms, but we managed to pack in our instruments & find a seat on the floor. For four & a half miles we jolted along in this fashion, then got out and had some dinner at the driver's house.

There were six in his family,—2 girls about 12, & 2 boys about the age of Roger & Bernard. Two rooms sheltered the unfortunate six,—one the kitchen, the other the bed-dining-sitting-drawing room. The kitchen was an ordinary looking kitchen. In the second room was a double bed, a table, a couch, a big trunk & three chairs; the walls were whitewashed but speckled with the results of many fly-hunting engagements; all round the rooms were hung shop calendars, except where two pictures of Mr & Mrs Paul Slocwzyk, in wedding garments broke the line. An R.C. image, an alarm clock, & a few pots of Geraniums in the two tiny windows finished the decoration & furnishing of the room.

Our dinner was a couple of fried eggs, mashed potatoes, coarse bread, & tea. When this was finished, Mr Slocwzyk growled something in Galician, & his wife, or her arm, shot onto the table with a big glass of cream & a bowl of strawberries. I think I ate about three pounds of strawberries, because the bowl was twice filled. Have you had many at Ponemah?[1]

After dinner we got to work. We had to find the level of a piece of ground where a road is to be built. The Mink River cuts across the road allowance twice, as you will see by my skillful drawing. The 2 lines bounding the road allowance

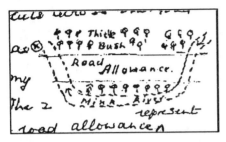

represent a barbed wire fence, which crosses the river twice. We had to put a peg in at the spot marked "x" & as Crowe cannot swim, I had the privilege of taking an axe & peg & chain (or steel tape measure), & swimming under the wire to the required spot. There, like an Indian savage, I chopped my way through a couple of yards of bush, & put in the stake.

On Friday I had a holiday & went to Dauphin Fair. I saw Baby Belle, a girl who weighs 580 lbs, & had my fortune told; then went to see some horse races. The races were pretty good, especially the last, which was a horseback race; all the others were trotting races,—the horse drawing a light racing car. In the evening I saw a wrestling match; Tom Johnston, heavyweight champion of Canada vs. the champion of Texas. Canada won, but the match lasted 44 minutes. There was a fine stock parade, & baseball, & innumerable sideshows, etc. Altogether I managed to squander $3.00, & have a pair of cast iron cuff links to show for it.

Milly is away at her sister's on the mountain, picking strawberries. As I told you before, I think she spent the winter with some relations in North Dakota, & came back a most idiotic caricature of a fashionable Yankee young lady. She had six-inch puffs at her ears, & a two-inch fringe on her forehead, & a most ludicrous walk, like the gait of a duck. She had, & still has, a piercing crow-like voice, notwithstanding which she attempts to sing at times without the slightest considerations as to tune. Even my musical instinct tells me that she is never within two whole notes of the correct one. These are the characteristics that first struck me when I was awakened one morning last May by her retailing the current gossip of Bathgate, N.D., to her mother. She is considerably improved outwardly now & I have discovered several good points. She is a good skater, understands baseball & hockey, &

best of all, she has a perfect talent for making lemon &
caramel pie...

Love from Bill

[1] A resort on Lake Winnipeg near Whytewold where she was staying.

Dauphin
Sunday 10:30 a.m.
24 July 1921

Dear Mother

...Mrs Bonnycastle loves to talk about any big questions
of worldwide interest, and keeps most wonderfully well-
informed on all subjects. I went over to her house one day last
week and found her absolutely alone,—the boys were all at
Russell, & the rest were out for a drive with some friends. We
began to talk, and from about 7 till 9^{30}, she was telling me all
about a book of sketches of the great British statesmen—not
at all in a pedantic manner, but very interestingly. When
Father & I went over for lunch last Monday, the two got
talking so fast over all sorts of questions from Canadian
education to Church Union, that I could not get a word in
edgeways, and had to resort to a game of tennis with Geoff.

Love, Bill

Dauphin
Sunday night
August 14, 1921

Dear Dorothy,

I have just returned from a Holy Roller service, and am
beginning to recover my breath and ease my aching sides. At
five to seven I entered the church—a bare, clean building,
with half a dozen rows of seats, an organ, a carpeted dais, and
a desk & chair on it. Four feeble old men were exchanging tid-
bits of scandal, three little kids were sitting on the front seat,
and a couple of women, with their families of grubby children,
were whispering loudly.

At seven, the door opened and piercing shrieks entered. Then a little kid, just able to walk, was more or less politely ushered in, a very masculine-looking woman helping him. The woman went to the organ, gave out a hymn, & commenced to sing. Without rising, the congregation joined in. Then the "preacher" entered, in plain clothes, & sat down on the dais. The kid climbed up beside him, seized a money box, and joined in the worship. Two hymns followed, & in the time that they occupied, the kid had managed to pull to pieces two hymn books, fallen over the edge of the platform onto his elbow, expressed its views on the event, been pacified, discovered the tin collection plate, and marched round the room dropping it at every second step.

A "session of prayer" followed. At every pause in the preacher's speech, one of the old dodderers would groan "Praise the Lord." "Praise Him," "Ah—ha—ha—ha." At length this ceased. A couple more hymns followed, a lesson, a hymn & a sermon. As the prayer, so the sermon was well punctuated by ecstatic groans, the goo-goos of some more children who had entered late, a fight staged by the same, and selections from the collection plate. The party in front of me, a man & woman & 2 youngsters, had brought their supper & refreshed themselves with slabs of bread & butter.

At length the sermon came to a climax; the speaker's voice was muffled by the ever-increasing murmurs; the speaker stopped; the groans continued, increased, gave place to the crying of children, and the congregation sank to their knees. A burley teamster, to judge by appearances, began to pray. What he said, I could not imagine, tho he was not 2 yards from me; but a mouthing, mumbling old dotard behind him continued his "Ay—men's," "Oh—aha," etc. The leader in prayer got more & more worked up, & more & more incoherent; the old man got almost hysterical.

The other, with his head doubled up on his chest, & his arms hugging his stomach, his feet crossed, his voice rising higher & higher, rocked himself to & fro, and almost sobbed in ecstasy.

At length, overcome by the Spirit, he sank on his chair, and the old fellow began to sing a verse of a hymn. Everybody joined in, & when the singing died away, he was found to be praying. He had no teeth, his tongue seemed to curl around his lips, as I afterwards noticed, & he held his hand in front of his mouth, so none had the least idea of his words. All, however, continued to encourage him with mournful groans. At length all the prayers ceased, another hymn was sung, & the meeting adjourned. The old man immediately jumped on me, shook my hand, told me it was a grand thing to be saved, & exhorted me to give up my heart. Then came the preacher, who hoped I would give up my life. After him, the teamster besought me to keep my soul. Thus, as a disembodied soul, I fled from the church, & never looked back till I reached 117 5th N.W., when I refreshed my soul with a piece of cake.

Love from Bill

AUTOBIOGRAPHY

Two Februaries later I telephoned Mrs Bonnycastle to ask if I might spend a few mid-winter days there, escaping the tensions of exams. In that blissful spell she happened one day to mention Rhodes Scholarships, for which two years later I applied, with the Judge writing a recommendation for me. How thin a line of coincidence has often led me to a huge decision! In this, Father's calling me to Dauphin, my friendship with the Bonnycastles developing to a point where I felt comfortable inviting myself there, and Mrs Bonnycastle discovering Rhodes Scholarships for me!

My next summer job lacked all romance and fun; I'm not sure why I took it. It was to occupy a deserted rectory on a Sioux Indian Reserve [near Griswold, Manitoba] of fugitives to Canada from the Custer disaster of 1876, and there to teach reading, writing and arithmetic to some thirty youngsters aged five to sixteen. The Indian Agent, Macdonald, had a house three hundred yards away. His wife provided me with meals, but I slept in the empty, ill-furnished rectory. I took a number of books there that included Milton's *Paradise Lost* and Farrar's *Life of Christ*.

Companionship there was none. I had no car and the nearest town was a railway stop twenty miles away across the broad and bridgeless Saskatchewan River, which was that summer in flood. Yet I enjoyed the children trooping to school any time after 6 a.m. and quite eagerly learning letters and figures, though we communicated in a hodge-podge of English and Sioux and the skimpiest of books and materials. There was no school available all winter, so the best use was made of the summer lessons. The young teenage girls learned most.

Sunday church was faithfully attended. On Trinity Sunday Archdeacon Thomas visited us for the day and delivered a very long sermon. Much to my astonishment, there was rapt attention throughout the sermon and the sentence by sentence translation by the interpreter. He had accurately decided when the audience had had enough of the Trinity and replaced the last half of the sermon with a dramatic account of last week's burning of a barn at the farm end of the reservation.

LETTERS

Griswold, Man.
May 15th, 1922

Dear Mother,

The Archdeacon & I were met at Griswold by Dainton (Rev. A.S. Dainton) about 8:15^{pm} on Saturday. We left our baggage at Dainton's and promenaded the town in search of James Macdonald, the Indian Agent, locally known as "Sioux Jim." We finally discovered him lounging at a street corner with 8 or 10 hoboes, & leaving the Archd. with him, went to the house of Mr Mott, the school master. We had refreshment there, & talked till 12, when Dainton & I left & went to D's boarding place. There we slept & had breakfast, & at 10 met the Venerable at the Mott's, took journey in a car, & started for the Reserve.

Round Griswold, the land is fairly flat, something like the Downs, tho' not so high in hills. Two miles south, we started to descend a steep road, & continued to descend for some 2 miles. The road winds about the bases of hills or through cuttings in the hills, (which are dense with bright green poplars, or else covered with scrubby grass & moss) so that we could seldom see 100 yards ahead. At length we got to the bottom of the valley, & came to the Assiniboine [River]. The water washes the underneath of the bridge, & a few days ago was flowing over it. All the road, however, beyond the bridge is covered for about a mile, & the water running over it falls with quite a noisy ripple on the far side.

Dismounting from our chariot, we crossed the bridge & after waiting for some time were able to enter a little white punt which a figure like Charon silently poled along from the shade of the flooded bush. After rowing for about 1/2 an hour by the side of the flooded road, we arrived at the foot of the hills on the other side of the valley. A fellow called Montgomery met us there with a buggy, took us to his home for dinner, then, about 3, to the Reserve in a Ford, back to his house for tea, & down to the river at 7. We crossed the flood again with Charon (his real name is Jim Macdonald, but he is not related to the agent), & returned to the Mott's where Sat. night's programme was repeated in every detail except that we had bananas instead of a more complicated desert.

The Mission church at the Sioux Reserve is quite large— holding circ. 70—but is not remarkable in any way. The congregation was more notable. Half the service was taken by the catechist, Mr Jo Itoye (pronounced and often spelled "Eataway"), the other half in English by Archd. Thomas. The organ was played by an Indian, Mrs Pratt & the jumble of English & Dakota words made the singing rather confused. The Archd. preached, his sermon being interpreted sentence by sentence into Dakota by Mr John Noel.

After the communion service, the Archd. held a meeting of the congregation, told them he had brought a teacher, and a very good one he was (ahem!), then asked all the Indians to shake hands with me as they left. "Hoc re gesta" (ask Moll,—ablative absolute).

We inspected the basement of the church & then the mission house. I elected to have the school held in a double room of the mission house. Macdonald (the agent) lives a stone's throw away, so I shall have meals with him & his wife, but sleep & study, etc. in the mission house. Until the camp bed arrives, however, I must put up at (& put up with) Macdonald's house.

I have seldom seen a finer view than the view from the spot of the Sioux mission. The hill slopes down gently to the plain in the valley. At the far side of the plain, a mile away, flows the Assiniboine, and its bank rises into a range of hills clothed with green young poplars and brown patches of trees whose foliage has not yet appeared. Now, the plain is flooded, the water being over most of the fence posts, & the view from the mission is like one of a Scottish loch, with the abrupt hills. From the Griswold side, the sloping downs make it look like the Sea of Galilee.

Moll had better come out here for a week or two in July, or come out now, & let me coach her for her exams. The mission house has 9 rooms, so there would be plenty of space.

I should have gone out to the Reserve today with the Macdonalds (who spent the weekend in town) but they started before I was ready, so I am waiting now for Charon to ferry me across to the dusky land "whence there is no return." Work does not commence till Monday, May 21st, so I shall have a week in which to make arrangements for lodging, & to get to know the people, etc.

With love from Bill

Address: High & Mighty, Great & Glorious
          % Indian Agent
          Griswold, Man.

Sioux Mission
Griswold
May 28th, 1922

Dear Fambly,

I suppose you are all wondering how I have got on with my school teaching, and how I like it, etc.

My bed and effects arrived in Griswold last Monday (22nd) I think, but owing to the flood, I was unable to get it to the Mission House till yesterday. Yesterday I got a livery man to bring it to the Griswold side of the flood. The Macdonalds have now a boat, so I rowed them over on their way to town, & returned with my bed. It is now set up in the Mission House, & I have only to sweep out the room, set up a wash-stand & table, & lay me down to rest tomorrow night.

Last Sunday, I got Mr Jo Itoye (the catechist) to announce in church that on school mornings I would ring the church bell at 8, & expect every child to be present at 9. Accordingly, I got up early & rang the bell, & at 8³⁰ saw kids assembling. At 9 I rang the little bell, the kids entered, & I began to take their names. The first few were too timid to answer, or did not understand me, so, thought I, I must show my resource-fulness. "Token eni cyapi?" I said—this is the Dakota for "What is your name?"

A very audible titter ran round the room. Just then an old Indian put his head round the corner. I was not a little surprised to see a wholly unbidden visitor, but managed to make use of him as an interpreter. I had got most of the names when 2 little children appeared, Abraham & Willie Mini. I got them seated, when another Indian put his head round the door. He paused, looked furtively round the room, entered, & leaned against the wall. "Good morning," I said. "Ho!" Having thus exchanged greetings, I turned to Abraham & Willie. They looked very bashful, & evidently did not understand a word. I turned to the visitor, & asked who they might be. In a very gruff voice—he was well over 6 feet—he grunted "Huh! these Mini papoose." I did understand him then, but decided that he had better get out & leave me to my work, so I took no further notice of him, & after loitering a few minutes to exchange salutations with the boys, he departed.

Teaching is very tedious work. Two of the children can speak English, about 5 understand it, & the rest (there are 17 in all) don't know a word. I have 4 grades to teach, of which the 1st is composed of 8 kids from 6 to 10 who, after a week's patient toil, cannot say the alphabet as far as G! Grade 2 has only 2 members, a boy and a girl who can read words of 3 letters, but do not, I believe, understand a single word they read. Grade 3, 3 boys who read without a spark of meaning or life in a high-pitched monotone, with incredible slowness. Grade 4, 3 boys of whom I have some hope.

You may easily see that it is hard to keep these 4 groups at work. If ever a pupil does know an answer to a question, be it but "yes" or "no," he drops his eyes, twitches his fingers, glances to right, glances to left, lowers his head, & after a minute's dreaming, mumbles inaudibly into his shirt. I cannot yell at them because they get alarmed & stay at home thereafter! Since a Roman Catholic child cannot be compelled to go to a Prot. school, the Prot. parents seem to think it unjust that their kids sh^{d} be compelled, & simply cannot be made to send them. So I have a hard job to keep good discipline, let alone instill learning.

One day one of the boys, Jacob Blacksmith, apparently fought with one of the girls. Next morning the girl's mother presented me with the following note, written in pencil on a dirty cashbook leaf:

Say I wanta to say some thing at school the boy ar no good we thing boys ar to side and girls other side. Gecob girl tuck him all the thim can you look after the girl. the take roller stick [i.e.; ruler] any Ellen an is she cry home pleas will.

Jacob has not shown up since, so I have not made use of the roller stick!

I have been rowing a lot, & shooting a good deal, but the work last week I found most exhausting. Next week it will be better, I think. Excuse the scrawl. (Eaton's goods arrived Sat.)

Bill

Sioux Indian Reserve   Sunday
Griswold   July 2nd, 1922

Dear Father,

It is just bedtime, and I have been up till 2 a.m. the last 2 nights! but I cannot break my rule—write home on Sunday.

For the last hour I have been worried with the hoots & whistles of some wild young Roman Catholic Indians. I am sitting upstairs. At last I determined to go down and shut them up. I walked out of the front door, & round the side of the house, & came across a young man climbing out of the basement window! He seemed alarmed at first, then appeared very affable & patronizing till I cut him short very rudely. He could not, or would not, tell me his name, but I got a by-stander on the hilltop to tell me. This is the second case of housebreaking this week, & I will let Macdonald handle it this time.

The Inspector visited me last Tuesday & I had a night-mare of a time. However, he saw the need for kindergarten equipment, & will send some soon. This being his first visit to an Indian school, he seemed at a loss what to think of it, but I fear his impression was far from favorable.

The box & clock reached me on Friday. Many thanks for it all, but please keep account of it, as I shall want to square up when my pay comes,—about July 15th, I hope.

Miss Havard, the former teacher here for 7 years, is helping me very generously. She is on holiday from the Industrial School at Portage, but hopes before long to get on to an Anglican day school. Perhaps you will get a letter, or visit from her soon.

Love from Bill

[To his family]   Sunday, July 9, 1922

...Talking about letters, the following is what a 12-year old produced when I told him to write to Miss Havard, the former teacher here:

Dear miss Havard
     oak Lake is a good sport, and Indian is a football tim.
Dear miss Harvard
     it is no hot today. It is a coal today.

We had a great scare last Monday. An Indian travelling from Dakota developed small pox last Sunday in Brandon. It was feared that some of the Oak River band might have come in contact with him, & returned to the Reserve,—in which case all of us must be quarantined & vaccinated. To add to the general misgivings, a squaw with sores on her face persuaded herself that she had small pox, & came, attended by quite a crowd, to the agency. She turned out to be quite free from it, but Monday was a somewhat anxious day, not relieved by the "tum-tum" of Sam Synaka (medicine man) which rattled about the hills from dawn to dark, & dawn again. It turned out that the case at Brandon had met none of the Indians, so we are quite free from restraint.

I got the organ carried over to the Mission House after service this afternoon, so I shall get better singing, & more practicing this week.

I hope to spend next weekend with (Rev.) Mr. Hatter at Oak Lake—the next town west on C.P.R. [Canadian Pacific Railway]. I met him at the Sports last Saturday (July 1st) & like him very well, & am delighted with the town—so neat & clean & prettily treed, & such a refreshing air of good fellow-ship after the vile atmosphere of Griswold, thick with a thousand mean whispers from every one of its 300 contemptible gossiping busybodies.

The small amount of reading I have done in comparison with the length of time I have been here quite disgusts me, &

I really think I <u>ought</u> to stay here from the 24th to the 29th.
—However...

Love from Bill

Sunday night, 9¹⁵
Aug 7th, 1922

Dear Mother,

I am delighted to hear of the number of fine books you are
reading, & am glad Moll has begun a <u>book</u>. Dorothy, it
appears, has not yet emerged from the "Lickle Tickle" stage.
By the way, I intended to write this letter to Dorothy & thank
her for the dollar which she sent me on June 15th. I suppose,
however, that it will be safer if I put it in your hands.

Last Tuesday I was visiting, & happened near the "teepee"
(house) of Harry Hotán, medicine man. All about his place is a
dense grove, of Manitoba maples, I think. I was walking along
the trail when I was startled to hear a number of men's voices
suddenly break into a rude chorus, swell, & die away. I peered
into the depths of the bluff. I saw nothing. At last I discerned
a low, dome-shaped tent, & detected a low voice inside. I
hesitated what to do. Should I go in? As I wavered, I heard a
rig approaching, & not liking to be seen gazing thus, I passed
on. Today a Christian, John Noel, described the doings inside
the tent, as he has been told by a participant. A hole is dug in
the ground, & 4 stones, heated white-hot, are thrust in. Water
is poured on. The effect is their "god," and they worship him
with songs and incantations. The ceremony, I am told, is fairly
frequent, so I shall get another opportunity of investigating.

Love from Bill

Sioux Mission
Aug 13th, 1922

Dear Bublumsquik[1]

How do you diddle di dee? I wrote a hurried note to
Father yesterday, but reserved the news for today.

About 12 o'clock yesterday, I ascended my velocipede, and
descended the hill. After a long journey of 11 miles under a

hot sun, I reached Alexander, & got dinner in a restaurant. I then called on Mrs King, & spent some time talking there. Then we went downtown; & after getting my hair cut, I proceeded to the [grain] elevator where Mr. King was working. He showed me over the whole building, from the engine room outside and the machinery in the basement, to the topmost floor, where the wind whistled through the windows, & nearly blew me overboard, *je ne pense pas*. After having supper with the Kings, looked at the War Memorial, & the Anglican Church, & saw the fine little organ which Father consecrated in 1920 (?). Clouds were now gathering in the west, & lightning flashed occasionally, so I hurried away. I expected to be forced to take shelter at every house, as I was riding right into the storm. When I got onto the Reserve, lightning was playing across the whole heavens from every side, & above me I heard "the roar of heaven's artillery." The air was stifling, & perspiration rolled off me freely, but no rain came. I pedalled as hard as I could, & reached the foot of the hill. A big puddle of water lay there, but I grabbed my bike and jumped it, then dashed up the hill. I left my bike at the Agency, then ran across to the Mission House, & as I closed the door, the rains descended & the floods came. Not having a lamp, I got to bed at once; but 3 times I sprang up, thinking the Agency or School had been struck. Half a dozen frogs, who were camping for the summer months in the basement, set up a piercing whistle, which twice made me start up, thinking I heard Macdonald whistling for me to come & help him save his burning house!

On Wednesday, Griswold (undenominational) Women's Missionary Society had a social up here at 7 o'clock. I was engaged in flinging handfuls of frogs out of the church basement when the first visitors approached. I hurriedly swept the remaining dozen into a corner when I observed them, then hurried across to the mission house. About 30 visitors came, & I showed them over the school, & put up with usual inane remarks: "Isn't that splendid!" as the old ladies contemplated a page with ink spilled over it! A Miss Simpson gave a short address on work in a Chinese school, but her voice was very feeble and her words not eloquent. However, she showed us a number of very finely wrought models of rick-shaws, & ploughing, & fishing, & sedan chairs, & a coffin, etc. The evening passed very pleasantly.

Attendance at school last week—11. I shall be glad to get back. My brief visit to Alexander afforded a delightful break from the monotony of the sights & sounds of the Reserve.

Love to all from
T. G. M.[2]

[1] A pet name for Dorothy.
[2] The Great Man.

— IV —
"FEED THEM BLEEDING CATTLE!"
(May—June, 1923)

AUTOBIOGRAPHY

In my Junior year [at the University of Manitoba] I did some debating, and organized a volunteer morning student chapel service which went well. I also read an evening lesson at St. Luke's and worked at my small Greek and Latin classes with pleasure and success, all due to my early grounding in Belfast under Mr Gee. Especially I liked writing Latin compositions, studying that masterpiece of skilled instruction, Bradley's revision of Arnold's *Latin Prose Composition.*

It was a rather dull year until Mrs de Pauley sent me a clipping from the *Manchester Guardian* pasted on a penny postcard with the message "This may interest you." The clipping announced that a scholarship was available at Keble College, Oxford, to the sons of English clergy. "Apply immediately," it said. I did so at once, for the deadline was about three weeks away.   My father said he could not possibly send me, but I knew that cattle were newly being admitted to the English market, and I asked Norman Young about it. He was a senior student who afterwards founded the Ravenscourt School and lost his life in World War II on the fatal cliffs of Dieppe. He explained the method of going to the stockyard and volunteering to escort cattle by train and boat without pay, but with a return trip contracted.

A few days later, about 5 p.m. and in my oldest clothes, Father put me on a fairly long cattle train with a cargo bound for the inland town of Manchester, which was approached from the sea by the Manchester Ship Canal. Once a day we four cattlemen must detrain our cattle at sidings to water them, and drive them back into their boxes, where we must also feed them hay. Our speed was perhaps 30 m.p.h., and was often stopped when an important passenger train must have right-of-way and we must creep into a siding and wait till the Trans-Canada roared by. Sometimes we stopped at small towns to buy provisions or berries from young Indian pickers. In uninterrupted passages the easy roll of the freight train invited one to walk the length of the cat-walks and converse with the engineer and fireman who seemed to welcome a visit. My fellow cattlemen were rough but congenial.

LETTERS

May 31, 1923 Just past O'Brien
P.Q.

Dear Mother,

I am sitting on the platform: the wind is strong, the speed is good, the springs bad, & the writing consequently illegible.

Last night about 9 we reached Cochrane. There several loads of cattle & pigs, & their crews parted from us to go S. to Toronto. We saw that our cattle were fed & watered, then pulled out about 1^{30} a.m.

Only 6 of us being in the coach, we each had 2 seats, & took cushions from other seats to make up a bed. With my coat for a pillow, & covered with the brown blanket, I slept like a log until 7, when we reached the French village of O'Brien. Waited there about 2 hours & got apples at a restaurant (excellent) & got 10 cents worth of milk from a garçon returning from milking (also excellent).

I enquired about a vest-pocket camera here, & finding the price to be 6^{50}, bought one. I wish that I had brought my own with me, but this must do. I will keep it, & on my return, give it to D as a birthday present. But don't tell her yet, please.

Among the rough crew who left us last night at Cochrane was quite a decent young fellow from N. Sask.—Charlie Bailey. He lives near London, Ont., but was installing electric light plants in the farms out west. He has asked me to drop him a line on arrival in Eng., which I shall gladly do. By the way, a young Englishman of our crew, Bill Sykes (quite romantic!) has asked me to stay with him if I have any delay in Manchester; his home is there. Tom Myles, an old Scot, has likewise invited me to stay with him near Glasgow. I shall probably not have time for either visit, but I should not mind the experience, & I am greatly pleased with the Spirit.

Walker, the wit of our company, is fairly old—55, perhaps,—an Englishman who has been in business, in the army, a commercial traveler, & a writer for papers & magazines. He has an endless fund of funny stories: "An Englishman & a Scotchman got on to a tram. Soon a young lady entered. The Scot raised his hat to her as she passed, very politely. When she sat down at the end of the car the Eng. whispered to his companion, would he not introduce him to her? 'Bide a wee,' said the Scotchman, 'wait till the conductor comes round. She's no' paid her fare yet'!"

This morning our Scotch friend Tom Myles (whose diminutive frame is enveloped in Father's khaki shirt & pants) began to sing (?) Scottish airs. Walker joined in with a lusty howl at odd intervals, but finding this would not stop the singing, laid 2 boards on the floor of the coach, & by stamping his feet in alternate spaces, then kicking them up in the air, all the while emitting wild screams, gave us an imitation of a highland fling. It was most ludicrous.

I have just read a characteristic article by him in *The Toronto Sat. Night*, April 21st. Quite good. Sleep now. Hope to reach Q by midnight.

100 miles from Quebec
7 am Friday June 1, 1923

Dear Mother,

We had hoped to reach Quebec at midnight, but being delayed, were resigned to not arriving before 9 this morning (Friday).

We were playing whist till 10 last night. I was very sleepy & wrapping myself in coat & blanket, with holdall as a pillow, fell fast asleep.

The country here is very rocky with pine-clad rounded hills & innumerable small lakes of enormous depth (one of 3 miles in length, when sounded with a 12,000 foot line, showed no bottom! They are well-nigh bottomless). The railway skirts around these, often on a ledge which has been blasted & hewn out of the hills. Thus on one side of the coach you see a frowning precipice, on the other the exquisitely lovely little lakes with piney slopes beyond enclosing them. The railway is seldom any considerable height above the water, usually practically on a level.

Now the precipices are nearly all of a slate-like rock formed of great chunks, separated by innumerable cracks and fissures; they are not one solid granite mass. And this morning at 3:50, as the engine was beginning to take a curve on one of these narrow passages, the brakeman & fireman saw a great boulder the size of the kitchen table shake loose from its crevice, roll 40 ft. down the steep face of the rock, tearing the few saplings that stood in its path, & come to rest—a jagged block between the rails. This about 20 car lengths ahead of us.

The brakes were jammed on. But the front of the loco-motive struck the rock, the jagged corner of the stone was rammed into the sandy roadbed & the engine, striking an upper corner, by its own momentum was levered off the rails, carried over the stone & deposited in the roadbed, where its wheels, after ploughing up a few yards of ground & crushing the sleepers [ties] to match-wood, stuck fast. The engine was standing at an angle of about 45º over the water like this:

The 3 men in the engine could not jump to the left because they would jump into

the wall of rock, nor to the right, into the narrow embank-
ment of rough boulders or the water. They clung to the engine
& were saved. Of the train, the first two boxes (empty) broke
couplings & plunged into the lake, where the ends of them are
now submerged. The 3rd (also empty) likewise broke couplings,
but dashed into the wall of rock. The others were all un-
harmed & not derailed. Fortunately the cattle were all near
the rear (there are circa 35 boxes altogether), & so remained
unhurt.

Our coach, being next to the caboose (ie: last but one) was
scarcely bumped. I was awakened by a jolt rather greater
than usual, but took no notice of it till the news came from
the end of the train that there had been a wreck! Bill Sykes
slept thru it all.   Love from Bill

                                             Quebec, P.Q.
                                    Sat 3 pm, [June 2, 1923]
Dear Mother

We reached Quebec this a.m. about 10. Since then I have
been wandering up & down the quaint old town. Now (2:30) I
am sitting in my overalls on a bench near quay # 27, resting
in the shade.

The *Manchester Brigade* has been loading freight at
Montreal (about 5 hours sail up the St Lawrence). She left
Montreal about noon, & will get here about 5. Then we load
our cattle & spread our sails for the East-O!

Our history for the last few days in tablet form, is this:

Wed. midnight—parted company at Cochrane with those
who are bound for Toronto.

Thurs.—uneventful, Sleep, cards.

Friday—4 a.m., Wreck. At 10, salvage train, crane, etc.
We went back 45 miles to get food & water for cattle.
Laborious afternoon, 2—8^{30} piling bales of hay into trucks, &
driving cattle out to water & into trucks again. Supper. In
train at 10^{10}. Passed scene of wreck 4^{15} am, but again too dull
to take snaps. Very disappointing to twice miss such a
spectacle. As we passed this morning, the sun was bathing the

hill tops; another half an hour & the spot wd. have been quite light.

Immediately we passed the scene, I went to bed again. Roused, washed, shaved, packed up & ate a piece of bread & butter thickly spread with pork & beans, & another with peanut butter. Then wrote to Dave & Dowker.

Scenery splendid. The French Canadians are great on market farming, taking any amount of tomatoes, lettuce, cucumbers, et cetera to the great market at Montreal. The landscape is like English scenery—small fields, white cottages, windmills, churches. On my right, in a broad valley, rolled the lordly St. Lawrence, with a few vessels, like water bugs, on the great expanse.

There is a tremendous trestle bridge over the river shortly before you reach Quebec—the Viaduct de Coutage, or something like that. I took an instantaneous snap of the view downstream as we crossed. And when we halted in the middle, I snapped all the crew standing there, with a locomotive in the background.

At 11^{30} this morning I got my passport & money. I have lodged $\$38^{00}$ in the bank of Montreal here (as the Cunard agent preferred this plan to keeping an account with me) & have drawn the other $\$12^{00}$. $\$7^{14}$ I got changed into £1.10, the remaining $\$4^{86}$ I am spending here on meals, sight-seeing, films, etc. But for the expense of the camera, my original $\$10^{00}$ wd. have been ample.

During my peregrinations this morning I asked the way of 2 youngsters about 8 years old: "Où sont les grandes magasins?" "Oh, voici, en haut, voici." They piloted me from the lower to the upper city, showed me where to get "filmes pour faire tableaux" & most politely thanked me when I bought them each an ice-cream cone.

The streets here are mere lanes. Car tracks are single, like Norwood or old Maryland Bridge, & no vehicle can pass on the left side of the street car. The buildings are steep & crowded & high. No boulevards. Crooked streets. One street, the last in the lower city, is closed on one side by a 30 ft.

precipice, which faces the houses on the opposite side. But the big buildings are very fine & numerous.

The place is quite like Belfast. Across the river are dozens of small hills, broken & isolated but otherwise like Cavehill, looking across the lough—Must put ropes on the cattle now, before ship comes in.

Love from Bill.

PS: Wd you keep these letters for reference, if I try to write up my experiences on my return? My diary is, of necessity, sometimes scanty.

AUTOBIOGRAPHY

The accident for which we were easily blamed had caused the ship owners substantial demurrage fees while the ship lingered unprofitably at the dock; now every hour counted and the cattle must be instantly roped and led to lower or upper decks and there individually made fast, even in the semi-darkness. Some cattle were Texas long-horns; it was no joke to swing over their heads and adjust ropes to their horns, then fasten the ropes to stanchions. At last the desperate jobs were done and the cattle-men sank into their bunks in two cramped bunk rooms, each with fixed bunks, a fixed table and fixed plain benches.

By 3 a.m. the cook sent us two steaming pails of coffee, announced noisily, "Ere's your coffee, you bloody cattlemen! Get out and feed them bleeding cattle!" We were now at sea on the wide St Lawrence and ready to "muck out" the night's droppings, then distribute water and hay (which was carried by pitchfork from a hold far below). By 6 or 7 we could knock off and wait, in my case sleep, till breakfast came to our rooms at 8. The stench, filth, heat and rolling motion made hard work even harder, and dangerously hard for one elderly cattleman among us; I was glad he survived the experience. I "passed out" in one of the hay-filled holds, where the ship's mate saw and roused me to work, then kindly let me sleep the clock round. By then we were in the Straits of Belle Isle and I felt pretty normal in shining June weather.

A few days on and we saw northern Ireland spread in sunshine, then the Giants' Causeway. Late at night we anchored at Liverpool and next morning were steaming, silent and serene, up the Manchester Ship Canal. How blissful to see early postmen on their bicycles on country roads till at last we entered crowded, busy Manchester about noon.

LETTERS

35 Castle Road
Salisbury, Wilts.
Friday, June 15th, 1923

Dear Father,

As you may see, I am now at Auntie Bea's. I suppose a brief chronicle of my adventures since I sent that card by the pilot from the mouth of the St. Lawrence is what I shd. now compose.

Sat, June 3rd. Left Quebec, 10[30] p.m.

Sun or Mon. Dropped the pilot.

Tue. Wed. & Thurs. Desperately seasick.

Fri. Retained my food. Worked.

Sat. Appetite normal.

Sun. Sight of Ireland all day. Appetite abnormal.

Mon. Welsh coast in view at dawn.

Tues. Off Liverpool. "Lay to" all night awaiting tide to ascend the Mersey to the Manchester Ship Canal.

Wed. Up at 2[30] a.m. Cattle unloaded at a dock lower down than our landing place at noon (by longshoremen). Roamed the town for a couple of hours at night, but slept aboard, as we had not passed the Immigration Office.

Thurs. Up at 7. Breakfast at docks. Tram to town to present my London draft & wire home & to Auntie Bea. Informed at Cunard Agency that they had received no advice about this draft. Therefore, I must leave it while they inquire. Returned to docks. Passed the authorities. Returned to Cunard Agency (in rags,) expecting immediately to draw £31 odd. "Neither this office, nor the Liverpool one, has received any advice of this draft. Until such time, it is worthless. Leave it here & call at the end of the week!"

I had about 6/3 [6 shillings / 3 pence] on my person, plus boots minus heels, khaki shirt (worn day & night for 17 days), blue pants (frayed, faded & out at the knee, suspended by knitted tie knotted round my middle), aged Canadian winter cap, with ear flaps, borrowed from Walker (my own having been stolen) & my overcoat, stained & fringed with ragged ends of the lining which dangled about my legs. I had attracted amused notice from the passersby on my way from the docks. I was condemned to the same ridicule for the rest of the day, & endured it as best I could—Luckily I had sufficient money to wire Auntie Bea for £7, but that sum did not arrive till a quarter to five, & I was homeless till then. A chance meeting with 2 of the cattlemen about 2 p.m. provided me with a charity dinner—At 4^{45} I got the £7, & before 6 had bought a suit £3-3-0, shoes 25/-, socks 2/6, 3 collars 2/6, hat 10/6. I then got a bath at the Y.M.C.A. & left for Salisbury at 10^{30} (ticket 25/11).

I reached here 8^{20} this morning, walked up to 35 Castle Rd.,[1] saw Auntie Bea, had a real civilized breakfast of porridge, boiled egg, bread & butter (homemade bread!) & lettuce, radish & cress—off the old Charlemont china.

Monday next to Sat I expect to spend in Oxford—still on borrowed money, which I most heartily abhor & resent.

My contract provides me with free passage, no work, on the "Brigade" again, leaving Manchester June 28th. From Quebec or Montreal I shall get 1/2 a 3rd class fare to W'peg. I fancy that I shall need an extension of my 2 weeks leave here, however, & if so I shall make every effort to do so; there is reasonable hope of success.

I now feel clean, refreshed, & happy. Except for the seasickness, & the experiences of yesterday, the trip has been one of unalloyed interest, pleasure, adventure, & incomparably more valuable than a dozen such in first class saloons. Now for the important & delicate & difficult parts. I pray earnestly that I may succeed.

The Warden of Keble (Dr. Kidd) wrote a friendly reply, the burden of which is this; I am ineligible for the Squire Scholarship (because not domiciled in England). But I had better make an appointment with him by letter, & talk over affairs.

Love, Bill

[1] The home of "Uncle John and Aunt Beatrice" Watson, old friends from County Tyrone, who had retired to Salisbury, to be near their doctor son, Hubert. With them had come their daughter, Kathleen, who joined the staff of the celebrated Godolphin School.

— V —
"I'VE COME TO SEE THE MASTER OF BALLIOL"
(June—July, 1923)

Salisbury, Wilts.
17-vi-23

My Dear Mother,

Sunday morning, 9^{30} on the borders of Salisbury.

I am waiting till it is time to go to morning service at the Cathedral at 10^{30}.

The Cathedral is the pride of the country side. It was built about 1220, but the magnificent spire was not added till 1330-40. The top of the spire is no less than 404 feet above the ground! It is visible for miles and miles. The inside of the Cathedral is very lofty & splendid, but the light is somewhat harsh, for the building at present lacks those "storied windows, richly dight, casting their dim religious light." But there are any amount of graves with figures of the occupants lying upon them—one is an ancestor of ours, one Sir John Cheney, who died in the 14th century. This morning I will copy some of the inscriptions. Then there are little chapels & altars & monuments, and choir pews of the 13th century. And dozens of the stone flags are inscribed with the names, etc. of those who lie buried beneath them. In most cases, the passage of thousands of feet for seven centuries has almost obliterated the inscriptions.

What struck me as most delightful were the cloisters. The actual alley-way is of stone flags, & is about 20 feet wide, and quite lofty. In the centre is the most perfect green sward, and in this are 2 splendid old cedars. When Hubert & I went to see the building, light rain was falling from a dull sky, & the sight of the vivid green carpet, the sombre & solemn old cedars, the fine body of the Cathedral, and the towering spire, which soars aloft to an immense distance, was a sight for the gods. Then there is the chapter house, a circular building, with a very slender column in the centre, which at the top branches out to form an exquisitely vaulted roof.

Running around the walls, about 12 feet from the floor, is a quaint & ancient sort of stone frieze. It depicts Biblical events from the creation to the deliverance from Egypt. Among the other scenes, I recall the fall of Babel (it looks like the overthrow of a toy house of bricks), and the drowning of the Egyptians in the Red Sea, which is the last panel.

Tomorrow I set out for Oxford via Stonehenge. From Oxford I shall cycle to Herne Bay, take a train back to Salisbury, visit Escot (probably by cycle), then return to Manchester.

I am still horribly embarrassed over the money. Hubert is very willing to lend me all that I want, of course, but he is going to Switzerland with Kathleen on the 28th, and I know that it is putting him out. I shall not soon forget the horror of that day in Manchester, & tho' I have the kindest of friends here, who are willing & able to lend me anything; it is most humiliating, as well as perplexing. Half a week has been wasted already. However, it has been a very pleasant half week, & prospects are bright.

Love from Bill

AUTOBIOGRAPHY

I was on my way to Keble College where I hoped to see the Warden, the Rev. Benjamin Kidd, and apply in person for the advertised scholarship "available to the sons of clergy," so in a few days, riding dear Uncle John's huge and rather rusty Irish bicycle, I began one afternoon to pedal the 60 miles to Oxford. The land was beautiful and I pedalled up the long hill that leads past Nether Wallop, Middle Wallop and Upper Wallop till I stopped at a pub mysteriously named a "Free House:" untied, that is, to any one brewery in its sale of drinks. I had never

tasted beer and was far too cautious to begin now, so had a
simple supper and bed and breakfast, then rode on with some
excitement to find Keble College and meet Dr Kidd. Keble
seemed to be a stupendous brick building in which with high
hopes I found the study of Dr Kidd and explained my errand.
His manner was kind and surprised; he told me with sympathy
that I was not eligible for the scholarship since its terms limited
it to "a son of a clergy resident in England." These terms could
not be printed in the brief notice of the *Manchester Guardian*
but he was powerless to alter the terms and they must unfortu-
nately exclude me.

I was of course stunned. I had, however, secured three
letters of introduction from three Manitoba professors who had
attended Oxford, addressed to the heads of Brasenose College
and Oriel College and Balliol (pronounced "Bay´-li-ol"). The last
was considered impossibly difficult of access because of a great
tradition of high scholarship, and of high standards of Scottish
students who had special scholarships there. An earlier master
had been John Wycliffe[1] and a recent one, Benjamin Jowett,[2]
eccentric and ambitious, who had raised its reputation immensely. A rhyme describes him:

> My name it is Benjamin Jowett,
> I'd like everybody to know it,
> I'm the master of Balliol College
> And what I don't know isn't knowledge.

I gained an interview of sorts at Brasenose and Oriel by
presenting my letters, but neither college could encourage me at
all. Should I then attempt the impossible Balliol? I rang the
Master's doorbell about 2 p.m. and when a maid answered it,
said I had a letter for the Master of Balliol [Mr A.L. Smith].
Doubtfully she let me in, took my letter, written by Professor
Chester Martin, upstairs, then returned to say I might wait in
the Master's study till he could see me. The upstairs large room
looked over the quiet lawns and trees of the quadrangle.

I was led to a room diagonally opposite the door and waited happily for twenty minutes when a diminutive figure, tousled and untidy, entered, rummaged at his desk near me without a word, and returned to the door. I took him for a servant. He turned and said to me across the room, "What do you want?"

"I've come to see the Master of Balliol," I replied.

"I'm going out for a walk in a few minutes," he answered. "You can come with me."

Shortly he returned with a hat and cane, led me downstairs and into the quad, then by a locked door into St Gile's Street. I don't remember a word being said. As we walked on St Gile's toward the park, a beggar stopped him to ask the time. Stamping his cane, he replied "I've no time to be telling the time to beggars" and marched on. I saw the beggar sweep a theatrical bow behind us and cry, "Oh thank you sir," as we walked on in frozen silence.

I suppose there was conversation as we crossed the park, but I cannot recall it. We approached a clerical figure in a straw hat, the Dean, I believe, of Christ Church, and their conversation must have alluded to me, as they glanced at me, but it had no significant effect and the Master and I emerged on South Parks Road. He asked me who was my favorite Latin poet. When I replied "Lucretius," he asked why. By the time I had answered, we had turned into Broad Street, and after more silence he asked "What will you do now?" I replied disappointedly, "I'll work my way back to Winnipeg, sir."

He asked sharply "Work your way back? What do you mean?" I then began explaining my cattle-train and cattle-boat and bicycle travels, whereupon he invited me in to tea with Mrs. Smith and a couple of daughters.

[1] John Wycliffe: (c.1328-1384), English reformer and champion of the people against the church.

[2] Benjamin Jowett: (1817-1893), Greek scholar and clergyman, best known for his translations of the dialogues of Plato.

FROM A LETTER TO HIS FATHER

24.vi.23

...Mrs Smith was likewise very eccentric, asking me such
blunt questions as "How old are you?" "Why don't you go out &
work now?" but ignoring any polite remark or question which
I ventured to offer. To make matters worse, when she offered
a plate of muffins, I, in my nervousness, fumbled them all, &
then dropped the one I chose to the floor, where the 2 halves
parted & rolled one to my right & one to my left, so that I had
to get off my chair to reach them! All the comfort she gave me
was a brief "Pick it up!" Then a fat young nephew of 12
months was brought in for inspection & admiration, so that I
had to sit & politely inspect & deceitfully admire, with my
jaws parted in a fixed & imbecile grin, for nearly 10 minutes.
Then Smith returned, perched himself on the arm of a chair,
told me he was glad I had made myself acquainted, had a cup
of tea & 2 whacks of cake, & then asked me to come with him
again.

This time we walked about the playing fields of Balliol,
then called on 3 other masters & tutors (all of whom were out)
& finally parted at 6^{30}, very cordially, for he unbent
considerably in the last hour, & even told me about some
young nieces of his whom we had met on the fields, and
pointed out several points of interest, e.g. the old rampart
where King Charles had posted musketeers to beat off Fairfax
from the old wall of Oxford, & the grove where Fairfax had
placed his artillery, as well as telling me how successful
Balliol had been in rugby & rowing & tennis, etc. for the last 4
years.

Now for the result. There is a ghost of a chance of an £80
scholarship if (1) the present holder withdraws (as Smith
believes he is), and if (2) I show any promise. The first
condition Smith will know very soon. If the holder is resigning
it, then Smith will wire me to come to Oxford at once &
present myself for a test exam. So now I am trying to work in
a flying visit to Aunt K, but keeping myself prepared to
answer a summons to Balliol. A test exam—in Classics at

Balliol! Could anything be more terrifying! However, (1) Smith is certainly interested and sympathetic, behind his gruff exterior; that he should spend 3 hours tramping around Oxford with me is tangible proof of that, and (2) even if I make a poor showing, it will be realized that I have yet 15 months before entrance, and (3) "our times are in His hand."

Love from Bill

In the waiting room at   Basingstoke Station,
Friday, June 29th

My Dear Mother,

    As you may see by the address, I am stuck at Basingstoke Station at 10^{30} p.m. on the way from Oxford to Salisbury.

    When I arrived [at Herne Bay], I inspected my mail, & found a letter from the Master of Balliol directing me to come up to Oxford next day (27th) and write the Matric. Exam in Classics on Thursday & Friday.

    I had Uncle John's bike with me, and rode it across Hyde Park from Victoria to Paddington. At 6 we left Paddington & reached Oxford at 8^{20}. I was in my cycling outfit, flannel trousers, a soiled shirt, and coat of Hubert's, but I rode up to Mr Gee's house, and with profuse apologies, begged the use of his bathroom to change in. He very kindly gave me all I wanted, & would have detained me to dine with them, only I thought it better to hurry off to college & report as soon as possible. I did so, & then went to bed in some trepidation as to the outcome of the morrow's exams.

    Sleeping in Balliol! What may be the history of my rooms I do not know, but my bedroom looked on to a mossy, sagging roof of red tiles, which covered a quaint, old-fashioned timbered gable. My sitting room was a delightful place too, with a good sized dining table, and a writing table and 2 luxurious arm chairs, one on each side of the fireplace. There was also a roomy bookcase, and a sort of dresser with cups & saucers & cutlery, etc., but alas!, the biscuit tin was empty.

    At 7^{30} next morning the "Scout," or valet came in, took my shoes, left me hot water, & showed me to the bathroom. After

a good bath, I got dressed, then went to the hall for breakfast.
The hall is a wonder in itself, hung round with priceless old
pictures. It is all panelled to a great height with light oak, &
has a fine oaken organ. The breakfast was first rate,—like a
hotel breakfast. After it, I called on our tutor, & got advice
from him, then went into the first exam.

AUTOBIOGRAPHY

Only about a dozen of us sat the ten or so papers, morning and
afternoon; the others all from English schools and familiar with
the day's routine. I was surprised to find we sat on plank
benches screwed unadjustably to the floor of a small lecture
room and must write on a mere plank table screwed equally
firmly in place and holding at intervals a pad of foolscap paper,
a bottle of ink and a quill pen! Cyril Bailey brought in our
papers, distributed them and left us. I read the questions and
did my best on the first: "Chaucer was the most English of the
poets. Discuss with illustrations." After trying the quill pen, I
wisely took to my own. The other candidates were younger but
more at home than I was and were at odds with each other, but
friendly with such a stranger.

[LETTER OF JUNE 29, CONTINUED]

I had also to write an essay, in 3 hours, on the subject
"Has modern invention increased human happiness?" Well, all
the 5 exams are over now, & the less said of them, the better.
I failed miserably in them all, as far as I can judge now, and
greatly fear that all my trouble at Oxford will not get me the
means of admission in 1924 which I require. However, I am to
return to Balliol next Wed. or Thurs. [July 4th or 5th] & I
shall know definitely then. Meantime, I shall pay a hurried
visit to Escot, then have a rest at Salisbury.

I have got from the Manchester Shipping Co. extension of
leave till July 12th. On that date, therefore I expect to sail
from Manchester on S.S. *Manchester Corporation.*

Here comes the train,—11[22]

Bill

FROM THE TUTOR FOR ADMISSIONS

Balliol College
Oxford
June 30, 1923

Dear Mr. Westgate

The College resolved to-day to admit you to residence in October, 1924, provided that in the meantime the necessary funds can be found to maintain you & on the understanding that The College itself will not be able to assist towards this end. I hope that it may be possible for you to come to us under these conditions.

Yours very truly
C Bailey

AUTOBIOGRAPHY

I spent spare time roaming Oxford or talking in the quad. On the fourth morning after breakfast, Cyril called me to his room and explained that I did not qualify for a Balliol scholarship, but said the college would admit me after I got my Manitoba degree. Perhaps I could interest a local benefactor in paying my way, or could I get a Rhodes Scholarship? I walked as if on air at being admitted, thanked the dear tutor (who subsequently became my regular tutor and mentor and beloved hero,) and then pedalled southward to Salisbury.

LETTERS

Herne Bay
July 28th, Sat.

Dear Dorothy,

This afternoon is wet & windy so I cannot go out for a ride to Canterbury, as I have done twice this week.

Yesterday about 4[30] I cycled to a tiny little old fashioned hamlet, about 2 miles this side of Canterbury, but off the main highway. You pass over 2 quaint little bridges, past 2 little cottages with mossy red tile roofs, then turn to the left, & see the village main street. On each side are curious gabled cottages, with upper stories projecting over the roadway, as if peering down to see "who's dat knockin' at de door down dere!" At the end of the road—one could throw a stone from one end to the other—is a gateway, with another old cottage bulging out at it, & inside the gateway is an extraordinarily pretty old Saxon church. Its date is 600 & something.

The shape of the plan is just oblong,—without transepts at all. You go in through a low little porch, heavily timbered with massive oak beams, & step into the church itself.

The floor is stone, but lots of the stone flags are inscribed, & one has a brass plaque let into it. The inscriptions are something like this:

HERE LYETH Y^E BODYE OF RICHARD
HARRIS OF Y^E PARISH OF SEYNTE
PETERE IN Y^E COUNTIE OF KENT,
GENTILMAN, Y^E QUEEN'S
FRUITERER, DECEASED MDCXIII

There was a funny, short little man with a white evening dress tie & frock coat who was showing visitors around. Three visitors were just leaving when I entered & the old man came up to me and asked me if I understood what I saw. "No," I replied.

"Well, up there, that stained glass is 14th century glass, & of course very valuable." He might have added "and very dirty." Then he showed me the sarcophagus of St. Augustine,—a great reddish marble chest, very curiously carved & decorated. The only other one like it is in Ravenna in N.E. Italy. There was also a very rude oak chair, called a "penitence stool," I think, which was set in front of the congregation, long ago before Holy Communion, so that those who had been notorious evil-livers might sit there & repent, & so be allowed to approach the holy table.

I happened to discover, from my guide's conversation, that he was, despite his dress, the rector. So I asked him if he knew Dr. Crawford of Folkstone, for I was his nephew.

"Oh Yes!" he said, "and you are his nephew? Have you had any tea? Do have some afternoon tea!"

I was quite taken aback, but I declined afternoon tea, as I had just had some. However, he then brought me into his house,—quite modern to look at from the road,—but within a trap door he showed me a most enormous, cavernous, stone fireplace which dated back to perhaps 1500 & something. In the top room of the house, the Black Prince's body is said to have lain in State before it was buried in Canterbury Cathedral.[1] I have seen his tomb there.

I happened to mention that I was going to Canterbury for service on Sunday morning. "Oh! Really?" he cried, "and will you come here for lunch?" I gladly accepted, so tomorrow I shall have lunch at Fordwich vicarage, where the Black Prince's body lay in state!

Love to all,

Bill

[1] Edward the Black Prince: (1330-76), son of Edward III. He was made Duke of Cornwall in 1337, the first duke to be created in England, and became Prince of Wales in 1343. A valorous knight, he was known for his black armor. Edward died before reaching the throne, but his son later became Richard II.

— VI —
"COULD YOU SAY WHEN I SAIL?"
(August, 1923)

FROM HIS DIARY

Bicycle tour through Kent, Sussex & London:

		Time	Cyclometer
1st Aug	Herne Bay	7.25 am	219.5
Wed.	Canterbury	9.05	229.3
	Ashford	11.00	245
	St Leonard's	5.0 pm	
	Pevensey Bay	8.45	294.4
		1st day	74.0 miles
2nd Aug	Pevensey Bay	12.0 am	294.4
Thurs.	Knightsbridge	2.0 pm	307.3
		2nd day	12.9 miles
3rd Aug	Knightsbridge	10.0 am	307.3
Fri	East Grinstead	2.0 pm	334
	Walthamstow	8.50 pm	384
		3rd day	76.7 miles

Aug 1st, Wednesday

Miss L. called me at 5. Left 7.25. Canterbury about 9. Exquisite ride to Ashford. Just before entering Brooklands I slapped my right hand to my thigh in a great panic to see my 50/– [shillings] in notes, & felt nothing! Lunch at Brooklands 1/1. Pressed on across Romney Marshes against fearful wind, thru Rye, Winchelsea and Hastings to St. Leonard's at 5. Called at 15 Bohemia Row [home of John Weatherseed].

At 6.30 I left and rode on thru Bexhill and then across
Pevensey Flats. Flats are flat (as one might suspect) & marshy
in places, intersected here and there by dykes, which take the
place of hedges. A few cattle and sheep graze in the enclosures.

At 8.30 (deep dusk) I arrived at Pevensey Holiday Camp
Bay, found bed and breakfast cost 4/6 and took a room (I had
5/6 1/2d on my person). After a short ramble, read the day's
Psalms, commended my weary soul to God, & fell asleep.

<u>August 2nd Thursday</u>
Awoke 7.30, read Green's *History*, Battle of Senlac. I would
like to have bathed before breakfast, but had no bathing suit
& only 1s.1/2d left, for I had paid my account in advance the
previous evening lest I should lose my purse & be unable to
pay debts.

After stretching myself,—the bed was dirty & dishevelled,
& the pallet & pillow stuffed with sticks, I think,—I chased
after some soap and had a cold bath and breakfast at 9.15.
Then cleaned my bike,—assisted by one of the boys, & a litter
of 8 puppies. About 10 took Green's Hist. to shore & finished
chap. ii, lying on pebbles in the shadow of a boat.

What a magnificent view! To my right, an immense
crescent of sand, whereon the silvery ripples were chasing one
another, or breaking with soft ripply laughter. Above the strip
of pebbles surmounting the sand, I observed 4 solid cement
circular bastions or block houses,—similar to those erected at
Folkstone a century since, to repel Bonaparte; <u>their</u> use,
however, I did not discover.

To my left, a similar sight, without the fortresses. In the
hazy distance, far out on the left extremity of the bay, one
could barely discern Bexhill, & one could but guess at St
Leonards & Hastings beyond there.

And here Caesar first landed perhaps! On these waves the
brave aquilifer leaped with his standard from the ship with
his dauntless cry, *Desilite, (inquit) commilitones* ["leap down,
fellow soldiers"]. Here, also, according to Green, William the

Conqueror landed in 1066, & "crossing this shingly strand, gave the countryside to fire and the sword." Yonder hill in the distance behind Hastings is the Hill of Senlac, against which Wm. led again and again his Norman hosts, till by a stratagem he pierced the stout ranks of the English, & penetrated to the standard of Harold, "the last of the Saxon kings," & on that summit "he sate down to eat and drink among the dead."

After reading for a while, I hired a costume, & bathed in Pevensey Bay. Tide was poor, but the bottom was of pure sand, & the water & weather perfect. How different the keen sea air here is from the Thames' tainted air of Herne Bay! As I waded in toward shore, I decided for the sake of romance, to imitate that old Roman aquilifer. True, I had a bathing costume instead of Roman armour, & a bit of seaweed served for a standard, & I had no boat to leap from, nor any fellow soldiers to exhort. However, I put a look of grim determination on my face, clutched my seaweed, leaped into the air, cried out in a stentorian voice *Desilite commilitones*, & gracefully desilited headfirst, till my head struck the bottom with a resounding thwack...

Having thus distinguished myself, & won undying fame, I hied back to my lodgings, packed my things on my bike, & at 12^{10} set forth on the Eastbourne Rd. After some 20 miles—19 on rotten roads—& passing through Hailsham, I reached Mrs. Neal's at 2.

I tried in vain to get Manchester Docks by phone (for I found a wire from Uncle E. awaiting me here, to say that I was wanted to sign articles at Manchester today). Her son, Osie, & I played 2 sets of tennis, then Mr & Mrs came out & we played 2 more (they vs. us). After supper Osie & I were left together, talked for 2 hours, then came up to our several bedrooms. Beside my bedside is a little jar of biscuits. What an excellent idea! To be introduced at home!—in my room! It's now 1^{20}. Help yourself.

Good night.

August 3rd, Friday

At 7^{30} Osie banged at my door to cajole me into a cold bath, but before the battle was joined I heard his little sister Lorna crowing. What music it is to hear the crows & chirps of a baby in her bath, while the sun streams in your bedroom window, & with it the soft notes of a pigeon, cooing in the distant wood!

After breakfast I borrowed a needle & thread, & O & I went up to my room. I had a large canvas patch of khaki which I hoped wd. serve to strengthen the seat of my flannels; & taking off the trousers, I laid them on the bed, & commenced to stitch. I sewed 3 large stitches, then stopped to get my second wind, & then lifted up the work for Osie to admire, & learn from. It was very mortifying to discover that the pants were stitched to the sheet!

After taking snaps of each other, I decided it time to move on, and at 10 started along the Horsham Rd. Cyclometer 307.3. Nothing eventful happened en route. After, say, 5 miles of poor road, I got on the highway for London & did not stop until I reached E. Grinstead at 2. There I got dinner & about 2^{15} started off again. About 4^{50} I passed through Purley and at 5 rode into Whitgift [School at Croydon].

How shall I describe my thoughts as I wandered round the now empty playground, & peered in to the empty rooms, & saw the same notices, the same pictures, & in my first form room, the very same immense black sheet of stuff, with history dates all down it, & on the top, in familiar chalk letters "River of Time?" That the River of Time has flowed or that the *annorum series et fuga temporum* has not failed of leaving its impress on me, that that impress has not been all that it should, that I would like to stem that flood, & sail back to 10 years since,—all such thoughts occurred to me. And there was some bitterness in reading the list of Univ. honours won by boys from Whitgift,—also that none of the names were familiar, save a note about Mr Morgan, while I must be content with a bare & grudging permission to enter [the school].

After seeing Whitgift, I rode down Cherry Orchard Rd. &
looked at "Calthorpe" [their old house] & Vincent Rd. &
Highfield School, & then started off for London over the
Lansdowne Bridge & past the corner where Mother used to
leave me on those wintry mornings of '12, and I had to
struggle on tearfully alone.

I passed near the Crystal Palace, & then thru Penge &
Lewisham & London Bridge. It was now nearly 8 & I was
hungry & dry. I got 2 glasses of milk & then continued the
hideous journey. From constant grasping of the handle bars
my hands were horny & burning. The stooping caused
considerable stiffness in my shoulders, my face was burning
with the dry, scaly burning of a long, hot day's exposure, my
feet were burning & aching & my legs were very tired. The
London roads are mostly of stone blocks, & tho I suppose
extremely durable, are yet very bumpy & cause considerable
vibration.

At about 1/4 to 9 p.m., I reached the "Barker's Arms," then
Grove Rd, then St Stephen's Vicarage. I was just turning in
the middle of the road when out came Uncle E.,—hatless with
his glasses perched on the tip of his nose, rushing to post a
letter. I hailed him & shook hands, & then went in to the
vicarage alone.

No one answered the bell, so I walked in the open door, &
found E. & B. at tennis behind. After greeting them I was
hailed by Aunt K. from the bedroom window & told to come
up. They had not been expecting me,—in fact they knew
nothing about me,—whether I was now off the coast of
Iceland, or at Hastings, but soon found me a room, & let me
wash, and gave me supper. At 10.30 I came to bed, the end of
a tiring but happy day. *Vale.*

August 4th, Saturday

Next day, after dinner, when I looked for a long read, & then
tennis, a great treat was proposed. Oh! We'll take our tea to
Epping Forest. Uncle Eddie wd. not go, so I was to go with
Aunt K. & B. & Emily! My Gawd. Then Aunt K. dropped out,

and I was invited to cut bread & butter sandwiches while B.
had a hot bath! I did so, & wrapt them up in newspaper, & at
3^{15} of a boiling day we 3 started. After 20 minutes walk we
came to the outskirts of the <u>forest,</u> an acre of dusty, patchy
gravel, then a few dusty may trees—sorry scrubs if sorry
scrubs ever existed, & so on: caked & gravelly land & sorry
scrubs. We walked & walked for 15 minutes, trying to avoid
running into a tramway on our right & another on our left, till
we ran into a highway in front of us with a corrugated iron
paling on the other side. Having thus traversed Epping
Forest, we sought a patch of shade devoid of newspapers &
banana peels, & sat down to consume our repast with the help
of some tens of thousands of black flies & 2 wasps. We
consumed it & 3 bottles of lemonade, & fared home again,
arriving at 5.

After tennis I searched for balls, 1 lost, & rolled court,
then had supper—ending with a nice plate of porridge. After
supper, washing up. I agreed to get tomorrow's breakfast.
Read in the church,—or rather recited from memory Is. 53 &
Eccl. 12. Too dark to read. Then looked up tomorrow's services
in the *Times* & read of Pres. Harding & his successor, Calvin
Coolidge. Bishop Gore to preach at All Saint's, a High Mass,
11 a.m.

I am in a bad humour now, originated by the silly baby
rule of this household, & aggravated by the knowledge that I
have been mean enough to be worried by it. 10.30 p.m. I shall
be very glad to get home, & not have to be so miserably polite
& so politely miserable.

<u>August 5th, Sunday</u>
I am writing this in Hyde Park near the Marble Arch & in
sight of the Hyde Park variety of orators. Listened first to a
stout, jolly sort of Indian appealing for absolute equality of
black, white, brown, yellow & red men. He gave a woman
interrupter several witty rebukes, but she persisted in being
laughed at. The Indian finally descended, with an appeal for
money. Crowd promptly melted away. Listened next to a

curious Cockney, with his nose out of joint,—literally & figuratively. "The mistake that Lenin made, what was it?" (Here he bent double, till his neck was on a level with his feet, but his face somehow writhed upwards). "The mistake wot Lenin made, if you want to know, I'll tell yer: He thought you was intelligent! That's the mistake wot Lenin made." I forget the rest of his speech—something about "tuppeny dams" & "I've wrote a book, yer know, with 30 pages, & no soft cover. Real stiff book back it has,—cost me £23 to do it"!!!

I passed up a Salvation Army group, & a religious revivalist, & attended a Mohammedan Indian, whose little platform was labelled "Islam in Andhia (?) Mohammedan." The fellow was small & swarthy, with a black beard & green turban, & always got too many syllables in the word "interpret." "It isn't my principles which is different from my friends here,—be quiet a minute, yunno,—but it's his interpeeteration wot differents, and that is not no difference!" The rest of his speech was equally profound & coherent, & I wd. have left at once, but for the argument which 1 Jew entered into with him; the Jew finally got permission to address the crowd for 2 minutes, but once ensconced in the pulpit, remained there for 20 minutes, heedless of the vicious jabs in the stomach from the Mohammedan, & equally oblivious of adjurations to "be brief, my friend." He got a good clap at the end, but talked rubbish.

Passed up 4 other groups & sat down to write this. At 2^{00} got #12 bus for Westminster Abbey & attended the 3^{00} o'clock service there. Visited Poets' Corner before I was hounded out; saw also grave of "Unknown Warrior." This rather quaint rhyme (is it by Pope?) is on the monument to Milton & Gray:

No more the Grecian Muse unrivalled reigns.
To Britain let the Nations homage pay,
She felt a Homer's fire in Milton's strains,
A PINDAR'S rapture in the lyre of GRAY.

Walked about Parliament Sq., got bus to "Elephant & Castle," & a 35 to "Barker's Arms," Walthamstow. Arrived home about 6.

August 7th, Tuesday

Sent wire: "Stonehewer, Salford Docks, Manchester. Could you say when I sail? Westgate, Stephen's Vicarage, Walthamstow." About 3^{20} reply came from Stonehewer: "Required be here Thursday, 9th. Stonehewer."

Afternoon tea by Lottie. How delightful!—but utterly wrong, that one shd. enjoy, by virtue of money & the accident of birth, the fruits of the degradation (to use too strong a word) of the other.

More practice. "Abide with me." Packing, dinner at which Aunt K. set on my plate 2 huge slabs of toffee for the voyage. She is the embodiment of generosity of this sort—a very lovely sort. Prayers. More packing. Wrote nonsense in B's autograph album. Arranged to cycle thru' London tomorrow, early.

When I came up to bed, Aunt K. came in & sat with me, chatting for a while, trying to further my comfort for the voyage. I enjoy her sweet maternal spirit thus displayed; it is Christ-like.

Lovely atmosphere now about this lovely vicarage. A softer, regretful tone is in every voice; more frequent expressions of "my boy" from Uncle Eddie & gentler softness in the words & tones of my cousins. Parting,—not absence,— makes the heart grow fonder.

LETTERS

> S. Stephen's Vicarage
> Grove Rd.
> Walthamstow, E17
> 8.viii.23

My dear Mother,

Tonight at 11^{50} I leave Euston, arr. Manchester 5^{15} & sign on there at 10^{30}. I hope we shall sail sometime on the same day. When I reach M'chester I will cable you to let you know

I'm sailing, & also, if I can learn it, the port of arrival. All being well, I should reach Quebec or Montreal on the 21st & W'peg the 26th.

I got up this morning at 6, had my breakfast alone, & at 7^{15} cycled down to the city,—past Bethnal Green Hospital. I rode more or less at random, & ended up at the Tower. Then I went along Cheapside to S. Paul's, & would have called at C.M. House, but the hour was only 8 o'c. I next went to the Houses of P. & took a snap of them & of the Abbey, & then visited the British Museum. I could only spend an hour there, & spent most of it in the Elgin room,—where are stored the fragments of sculpture from the now ruined temple of the Parthenon at Athens,—which fragments Lord Elgin removed a century ago, & sold to the British people. I took some snaps in there & also took a snap of the busts of the first 4 Caesars,— Julius, Augustus, Tiberius, & Claudius. These 4 busts are on pedestals, set in a corner of a long hall. As luck wd. have it, just as I was pressing the shutter release of the camera,— Dorothy's of course,—a short-sighted old gentleman bobbed his head to examine the sculptures. and—click!—I caught the living among the dead!

My next visit was to the MSS. room, where among other treasures, I saw the *Codex Alexandrinus* & a piece of the *Codex Sinaiticus* & other codices; it is chiefly in the light of these that Bible revision was undertaken in the '70's and 80's [1870's and 1880's]. I went to Euston sta. & bought my ticket for tonight, then cycled home, arriving late for lunch, at 2 o'c. at Walthamstow.

My trunk has gone off now, by the green grocer's boy, & my good suit of clothing with it. I am therefore now in my travelling outfit. I can assume that Solomon in all his glory was never arrayed like the great man is now.

My next communication will be tomorrow, I trust, from M'chester & the next from P.Q., & the next by phone, & the next in person.

Love from Bill

— VII —
"YOU MAY GATHER THAT I AM CONFUSED"
(July—November, 1924)

SMW

As Bill was in Winnipeg at the University of Manitoba in his senior year, there are few letters from him until he went to Toronto in the fall of 1924. Nor did he leave a diary. However, his mother kept one and occasionally mentioned his activities. He may have been a weekday boarder at the college, but he appears to have spent weekends at home, which always included church with his family. He also attended occasional theatres, a convention and a lecture. He spent nine days of a spring break at Dauphin, from which we have a letter, and in the summer made two excursions of several days to Stonewall to help with the haying.

He received his B.A. in Classics from the University of Manitoba on May 15, 1924. In the following summer he took part in rowing races, and on July 18 his boat won. He appears to have been helpful in the house and garden, even doing the ironing on two occasions.

From Rita's diary, one gets the picture of a close-knit family in which she had more to do than her strength allowed. There was some part-time help, but she seems to have been responsible for their meals, making clothing, doing all shopping, visiting friends, and even paying the bills, all of which was done on foot as they had no car. Most of her diary entries end with "v. tired." Despite all her chores, she also managed to read books, write letters, read Plato to Bill, help Moll with French, and play chess with Rex when he was not on his frequent travels to Indian outposts.

The following letter was written from 513 McMillan Ave., Winnipeg to his mother while she was at the Anglican Camp at Minaki, Ontario:

Sunday night
July 27, 1924

My dear Mother,

Just a note for the family as I consume a hasty supper at 10 o'c.

I spent Sat. morning gardening. I began by cutting the lawn. Seeing this, old Mr. Fyfe began to cut his trees. To keep up with him, I had to cut a few limbs off our trees. Old Mr. Gardiner yielded to his curiosity, & discovering his neighbour's energy, proceeded to mow his lawn. The general stir prompted Mr. Johnston to come out; who seeing the whole neighbourhood engaged in cutting trees, did his little best by cutting branches off his trees. Thus my original energy was multiplied four-fold. Finally Mr. Johnston gave me an armful of chard.

Dorothy's cooking has produced no ill effects yet. She put in the ingredients of brown bread on Saturday, and took out a melancholy bannock that looked like a potato-cake. It was consumed, however.

Do enjoy yourself. Take in all the picnics & launch trips & afternoon teas & dances & corn roasts & festivities you can. Before long I'll get a job on a threshing gang & earn perhaps $250. Then you can have another spree; but you must make the most of this one at the present.

Paddy misses you sadly. He slept on my bed in the thunderstorm; but when his fright subsided, he left my couch & ended his repose on the chesterfield.

By the way, I have marked some of the poems in that volume *Shakespeare To Hardy* with a little ✓ in pencil at the title. I think those are the ones you will enjoy most.

Love from all,
& especially Bill

% C.A. Shipley
Balmoral P.O., Manitoba
Sunday, Sept. 14, 1924

Dear Mother,

Very glad to get your & Father's letters yesterday. This afternoon I propose to ride "Tiny" into Stonewall to evening service, & back. The whole ride will be about 20 miles.

Twenty years old today! How vividly I remember slipping into my 'teens—when we went for a picnic over Cave Hill. 14 I celebrated at the Mitchell's house in Belfast; 15, 16, 17, 18, 19 in Winnipeg, and here I slip out again at Balmoral. This promises to be a very brilliant & glorious year—these words are for you only, Mother—and I have long looked forward to it. It is my last before I reach man's estate; and I mean to make it count, so that manhood will possess a good foundation, with good habits confirmed and bad eliminated. I have been, in truth, rather glad of this short period of idleness; for while I have been helping Mr. Shipley, I have been under no obligation to work all day, & have taken much leisure for thought. And a quiet, lonely ride this afternoon and evening will perhaps be better for me than a rush home, off to service, Sunday school, back late, & a weary tramp to the caboose after the fashion of last week.

I have received a note from Mr. Bailey, of Balliol College, saying that he had sent me the papers for entrance this Oct. because he had not been absolutely certain of my movements; that my admission would be allowed to stand over till 1925; that he hoped I would come as a Rhodes Scholar; and that he was pleased with the extra reading I had been able to do, & with my success at Toronto. But please do not speak of the Rhodes to your friends; for my part I place no confidence in that quarter; at all events, conversation at the tea table can do nothing but damage.

Quid Multa? Expect me home next Sunday, with about 25 dollars in my pocket. Walter, a Scotch boy here, has challenged me to a race on "Tiny," he riding a young driver called

"Topsy." I believe "Tiny" in spite of her 20 years will win. Now for the turf!

Love from your elderly son.

What <u>can</u> the girls be sewing for a birthday present? Ah! pincushions, of course.

FROM RITA'S DIARY:
Sept. 18 Bill came back from Balmoral.
Sept. 26 Bill left by evening cattle train for Toronto. "Regretful thoughts in bed."

POSTCARD TO HIS MOTHER

At a Post Office in Toronto
Tuesday, 3³⁰ p.m. [Sept 30th]

We arrived at 7^{30} this morning, jumped the train as it was passing a convenient street car line in the city, & with mutual regrets & handshakings, scattered to our several ways. Met Hum[1] at Trinity—what a glorious, majestic, stately old pile it is!—& met the Dean, Mr. Hodgins. Hum took me to the University, where I had a delightful short interview with the Head of the Graduate School; he has invited me to lunch at Hart House next Monday.

Am now going down to Watford—still travelling free!!! By great good luck I find that two carloads of cattle on our train are going to a farm about 10 miles beyond Uncle Alec's. You know the railroad passes thru' Uncle Alec's farm; so that all I have to do is to get on the sunnyside of the brakeman, & then suggest how nice it would be if he would just clamp down the brakes as we pass that farm, till I can alight. Never, I repeat, shall I pay for travel!! Have also discovered a place where they teach how to jump on horseback!

Trunk & books have arrived. Hooray!

W.W.

---

[1] Humphrey Bonnycastle

Tuesday night
Sept. 30, 1924
Toronto

My dear Mother,

Two hours ago I was hob-nobbing with blasphemous drovers at the stock yards. An hour later I was stretched lazily in front of the fire in Hum's study discussing Rhodes Scholarships. And behold me now at 8 o'clock in a stuffy office at the CNR freight yards, surrounded by a battery of telephones with shirt-sleeved operators writing out "way-bills" and engineers & brakemen popping in and out for oraers for the night's run. One thing, at least, this knocking about does not fail to teach—in all company to be at home, and—an old Greek proverb—"be surprised at nothing."

I have a good roomy chamber near the "Angel's Roost" in Trinity [College, Toronto]. It is square, with a bed, a plain table, & chair, two book cases & a fire place. The walls are respectably covered in a dull blue paper & the ceiling is tolerably clean. The floor is bare, & I must get, in addition to a rug, some curtains for my three windows. A good deep armchair is essential, into whose inviting depths one may dive, & from that retreat watch the ruddy flickering embers solemnly wink at one's dreaming eyes. Yes, a chair is indispensable when there is a fire of coals to enjoy it before. I would also like a better desk. And a typewriter & some more books. I think I will imitate Erasmus in my wardrobe: who, when asked what he would do in the remote eventuality of his ever owning any money, replied "First, I will buy some Greek books, & after that a coat."

I tabulate expenses thus:

Curtains	$7.00
Chair	5.00 (bought for a song at the college)
Table	20.00
Typewriter	40.00

And how I long for some fine pictures! You & Moll & D. must arrange to come E. next summer before I dismantle my study.

—Did I tell you on that card this aft. that I can get the M.A. in June by merely writing 3 exams, without squandering valuable reading time on a thesis; & besides, Mr. Brett has invited me to lunch for Monday. Here comes my engineer & brakey. "Ready, Mac? Caboose is all set. Pull out in five minutes." So I must forsake you, & hie to the company of my railroad chums. Hope to reach Watford Wednesday about 7 a.m. Father will be there.

Bill

c/o the Buchanan girls [cousins]
63 Thornton Ave., London, Ont.
Friday nite [Oct 3, 1924]

Dear Moll

I have only time for another hectic note to tell you where I am and why. I reached Watford at dinner time on Wednesday after various misadventures which annoyed but did not harm me. Father & I were practically alone with Granny till evening, for the Westgate colony was away for a funeral en masse. Yesterday, however, Father & I got out Uncle Alec's car—a Chevrolet—& scoured the countryside. Father is as happy as a mudlark when he is driving, though his course is usually somewhat serpentine. Every field has associations of his boyhood, & every person suggests a host of uncles, aunts, cousins, granduncles and connections to the nth degree—such catalogues as trail away into infinity. Not a soul within five miles of the "Fourth Line" (R.R.4) but claims kinship with us. I am thoroughly addled, befuddled and bamboozled with them all. I kept track, I think, of the first hundred, but the rest are not quite so distinct.

You should have seen Father yesterday afternoon. We were bumping along very rapidly when we overtook a lady. I suggested that we give her a lift, but he said "Oh, no—can't be bothered with them all; let her walk." Hardly, however, had we come alongside when he saw her face. "Holloa!" he yelled, leaning across me & brandishing his pipe at her as we whizzed past, "Holloa! Eliza!" The affrighted Eliza "started

aside like a broken bow." As for us, we were on the brink of
the ditch, & but for timely exertion on the steering wheel,
would have landed in a puddle.

We came up from Watford to London this evening about
6^{30} & were met by the Buchanan girls, with whom I will spend
the night (Father is a few blocks away, at Will Buchanan's) &
proceed to Toronto tomorrow morning. Uncle Alec has swarms
& clouds & clusters of young, squealing, mauling young imps. I
was of course lionised by them all, & when I sat down to read,
had Mary Jean, & Beulah & Palmer clambering up my legs &
probing my pockets with sticky fingers, clawing my ribs & feet
& head with pudgy hands or belabouring me with violent
kicks from their chubby pink toes. I had to take them out for
drives & help them pick up apples & sit beside or opposite
them all at meals, allow them all to sit on my knee, and
submit to all the other tokens of infantile approval.

Love to all, Bill

<u>Do</u> get lots of riding...—Say, every Saturday morning. I will be
jumping very soon & then will teach you.

Trinity College, Toronto
Sunday night, 5.x.1924

My dearest Mother,

It will not do to break my promise on this first Sunday at
Trinity, so I'll indite a hasty note before bedtime.

Father & I came up from London yesterday, but he
stopped at Hamilton at 2^{30} and has evidently been waylaid for
Sunday duty. I hope to see him tomorrow, & have him up for a
meal.

I got here about 5^{30} last evening, with a splitting
headache; so utilizing the dinner hour for cleaning my room, I
was fairly comfortably settled by evening. I called on the
Archbishop about 9 o'clock about my Rhodes application, &
enjoyed a chat alone with him for half an hour,—so much so
that my headache vanished.

I find that the prospects for the winter are very promising. My room is large & airy, opposite the bathroom, & with an eastern aspect. I promise you some snaps of it in the near future.

Attended Holy Communion today at 8 o'clock in chapel, & (compulsory) chapel service at 11. The girls from St Hilda's—known in the corridors as "the Saints," join in the Sunday chapel services, & it occurred to me how much Moll would enjoy their saintly company.

There are several freshmen—technically spoken of as "the worms"—but as I sit at the grads' table, on the dais in the dining hall, I do not think there is much danger of my being treated as one of them. If any one is rash enough to accost me as "a worm," aha! the worm will turn! I'll transfix him with an eagle eye, (or two eagle eyes, for that matter). I'll wither him with a contemptuous glance, I'll shrivel him with a stony stare, I'll burn him to a clinker with a glowering glare!

Tomorrow I shall begin work in earnest. My program, as I plan it, follows:

Rise 5^{00} & study.

Breakfast 8^{00}.

See the Dean, pay the bursar, etc. 9 o'c.

Buy chair & typewriter downtown, 10 o'c.

Go to varsity (about 3 miles off) & enquire about rowing 11 o'c.

Lunch with Mr. Brett, head of School of Graduate Studies, at 1.

Thanks for Moll's letter. Meals and everything here excellent.

Love from Bill

Trinity College,
Toronto, Ontario.
Tuesday, 7.x.24

My dear Mother,

I am going to write the briefest possible note to you, merely so that a letter to you will be the first use to which I put my new typewriter.

In spite of a large, quiet, and altogether splendid room, I am finding it desperately difficult to settle down to hard work. The volume of reading which confronts me is staggering; I am at a loss to know where to begin. Moreover, this Rhodes business is difficult to banish from one's mind. And undergrad life is so wonderfully alluring. However, before breakfast I make some progress, and in the later forenoon too. Shopping, some calls on new profs., rowing on the machines in Hart House, and a final plunge in the glorious tank in the same building, occupied my afternoon today, and some Greek drama before my study fire, will engage the evening. Last evening, after Father left, two fellows down the hall invited me to ally myself with them in an attack on cold chicken. I proved no coward in the fray!

Tomorrow I shall row in the bay, with the Varsity crew. Now to my ancient drama, and goodnight to you, Optima Mater!

From your affectionate son,

Bill

PS A goodnight glance at my exchequer reveals the fact that I have now a fortune of five dollars and as many cents. The fellowship will pay me say $160 in two weeks or less. If Billy Martin's $28^{50} comes through, please do not delay and, indeed, if you can spare twenty dollars, I would feel more at ease and would consider it a loan. However, all immediate dues are paid, my room furnished, etc.: so that should you be enjoying no more than your usual affluence, I shall quite relish the experience known as "sailing close to the wind."

WW

Postcard to "Miss Westgate"

Monday morning, 13.x.1924

Have just received two letters from Mother, with enclosures of
(1) I.O.D.E.[1] scholarship blank, and (2) cheque from Billy
Martin. I can tell you the latter has just saved my bacon! I
was at a very pleasant reception by the "Saints," i.e.: at St.
Hilda's, last Thursday night, met some very nice girls—for one
of whom my next door neighbor is afflicted with the amorous
passion! Poor booby!

Have just dismissed the laundryman, Mr. Jay See Wo, or
is it J.C. Woe? & now must hike to the Univ. to have a tutorial
hour with a gouty & violent old fire eater. He alternately leans
forward, nay springs up & thumps your chest, his fiery face
wreathed in smiles, and next moment "confound your imper-
tinence, and make up your mind, young man, that I'll not take
your Latin prose. Confounded nuisance!" & he thumps the
floor with his stick, and instantly subsides again into smiles &
chuckles & good humour! I can tell you he's a peppery old dog
but I am getting used to the breed.

Love from Bill

[1] Imperial Order of Dames of Empire

Toronto
Sunday evening, 2.xi.1924

Dear Dorothy,

Many thanks for that delightful letter, which I have not
yet received. I shall enjoy it tremendously.

I had old John MacNaughton as usual last Monday
morning for Virgil. He is an erratic old duck; he prepares
nothing; he is so far above his subject that no matter what
part of it you question him on, he can pounce down on it and
explain it perfectly. He frequently goes into a lecture room
without the faintest idea of what subject he should deal
with,—whether 1st year composition or 4th year Greek
comedy: he takes his place before the class and asks them,
"What do we do today?" Last Monday, as it got near the end of

the hour, I tried again and again to interrupt him, but he brushed aside all my efforts and would not listen for an instant: the more I tried to butt in, the louder and faster he would talk. So I thought, You poor idiot! this is your funeral, not mine; you may blather away till you burst! On and on he went, till in a sudden pause at 11:20 he pulled out his watch. "O! I say! you know! good heavens!" and without another word, he dropped his books on the table, wrung his hands together, seized a book for his next lecture, and fled out of the room. I tell you he is a maniac.

There is a very decent freshman in Trinity, on this wing, named Reade. He is huge in size, very well read, a good sketcher (I sat for him this afternoon and last night for a portrait in charcoal), plays the cornet well, and has a fine bass voice. There are such wretched and petty and puerile indignities heaped on the worms here that he finds it rather refreshing to find an intelligent companion who is not bent either on persecuting him, or on trying to escape persecution: so that he and I spend a good deal of time together.

He was in my room the other night about 1 o'clock, talking to me (then lying in bed). The door was slightly ajar, so that I could hear any footsteps coming down the corridor. I did hear someone approaching; the steps stopped at the door, and some one called out to Reade, "It is time you were in bed, my friend." I naturally thought it was Roderick or one of my facetious neighbors, and cried "Come in." But he merely fumbled at the handle without showing his face to me. "Come on in," I repeated, but there was no response. So I loudly invited the intruder to visit the devil: whereupon there entered the Dean of Residence!

Your affectionate brother,

Bill

Trinity College, Toronto
Sunday 9.xi.1924

My dear Mother,

Half past nine on a bright, fresh autumn morning at
Trinity. I have had a saunter up and down the drive and
across the turf of the park since breakfast, and now sit at my
table overlooking the grounds, with the City of Toronto in the
background.

I should like to have Dave Mansur, above all, with me
here. A great letter from him last Tuesday made me quite
homesick for the days of last year. I am invited there for
Christmas, & shall certainly accept.

The stamp of man at Trinity rather disappoints me. The
fact that almost all my work is done alone cuts me off from
much undergrad society; but there are very few undergrads
here whose acquaintance does not suffice without their friendship. Bonnycastle is the only one whose company I really
enjoy, & now he has been elected House-Secretary of his Frat,
& he's moved out of residence.

It would be nice to give you a sketch of some of the types
here, if only I had a light enough touch to do it. Arts &
Divinity men are clearly defined; the former by open scoffing
at much of the mummery to which services are reduced, the
latter by feeble efforts and ineffectual, to defend consistently
their beliefs. Both, of course, are alike in <u>not</u> doing the works
of God!

There is the "Bishop's Candidate," in the first place. One
wonders at the object of his candidature: is he a candidate for
Ridicule? or for Compassion? or for country living? or merely a
candidate for anything that he can get?—an education, three
good meals a day, the adulation of pious old maids? In caricature, he appears with a gawky manner, a cockney accent, a
brazen voice, a total absence of wit, and only that brand of
humor that laughs at such spectacles as a man sitting down
when no chair is set to receive him—a rather poor type of
humour and childish form of jest. And when his coarse
humour is provoked, he laughs like a fog horn. He believes all

the articles of the Christian faith, because he has not the sense to doubt;—and makes a virtue of his obtuseness! His childish mind has been caught by the romantic vision of the New Jerusalem—"the radiancy of glory and bliss beyond compare:" or his infantile ambition to wear a surplice & dog-collar, hood & stole: and he has progressed so little since his infancy that he maintains the same ambition today, for alas!, the same ends, no higher motives. He reads what is given to him, conscientiously but without mental digestion—his mental organs can only digest slops and milk,—"Mother Goose," "Eric, or Little By Little," "The Bobbsey Twins," and the parables of the Saviour in their most material application,—and cannot begin to feed upon the raw beef-steak of theology—the nature of God, and the nature of man. How can our Heavenly Father implant in us spirit and intellect, then stunt them both by saying "You <u>need</u> not investigate and explore: just read Matthew Mark Luke & John, and swallow them holus-bolus: in fact, it is really a little better not to rely on your own mind, for thus you escape many pitfalls."

You may gather that I am confused these days, & the confusion is not wholly pleasant, nor wholly agony. Reade & Gardiner & Roderick come in at night to pursue these abstruse inquiries, & one feels a great freedom of mind in thought like this. True, it would be folly to rule one's life by one's present thought: but after due consideration, if my conclusions run counter to the teachings of the Church, it would be un-Christian to shelter in fallacy for fear of the storm outside.

Fortunately Bishop's Candidates are a minority here. There are a few clever arts men, but they (perhaps wisely, but rather cowardly) accept the church doctrines from sheer apathy. They affect no religion, so that one expects none from them: and when one finds it, one is all the more gratified. I much prefer the religion of an English public school boy to that of the average theological student. But I do want to find the reality and depth of true religion: it evidently does exist in men like Father & de Pauley & Farrar, and enables them to be rather more than mere men. And so I would have it in my case.

Please do not think I am working off a stale essay on you: I know no one here for whom I feel respect combined with intimacy. I wish there were nice families here, or rather, wish I could have access to the many nice families which <u>are</u> here.

I have met several rather nice girls from St. Hilda's, but I have held back from the last 2 dances, & shall continue to do so for the next few. There is a splendid masquerade at Hart House on the 31st to which I shall certainly go if I find a good partner, & there is the Trinity Christmas dance. These two will do me for the term, I think.

The place is deserted now, as the few who remained over the holiday have mostly gone to church. I must now stop,—though I see I have said nothing worth saying, nor at all what I intended.

Your affectionate, if prosy, son

                                                          Bill

— VIII —
"SONGS & HOWLS & POKERS ON PAILS"
(November, 1924—March, 1925)

WESTGATE NEW RHODES SCHOLAR

Reginald Wilfred Westgate, graduate of St. John's, Class '24, was last evening appointed Rhodes Scholar [from Manitoba] for this year. It is particularly to Westgate's credit that he was selected from among six candidates, all possessing most excellent qualifications, according to the report of the committee...

(*The Manitoban*, November 21, 1924)

Trinity College

21.xi.1924

My dearest Mother,

About 10 o'c this morning I got a phone call, & was told that a telegram awaited me in the Porter's lodge. You cannot imagine my feelings as I read your words. Lucidity of thought seemed to vanish from me, & I retreated to the Chapel for a brief space. John Reade is the only undergrad I have told here, although of course the Dean of Residence (Mr. Hodgins) was my next confidant. The news will of course get out, & I am half sorry now that I did not let the Dean post the news on the board, so that the whole business might get out at once & blow over. The dean took me up & hugged me! and I could scarcely compose my face, from mixed emotions. I was out all day after that happy moment, & had dinner this evening with Southam at Wycliffe. I have received two other wires—one from Dave MacLennan, and one from Dr. Clark, Hugill, &

Tracy—"Hearty congratulations from the Department." Dave's was characteristic—

REJOICE IN WELL-EARNED TRIUMPH.
ACCEPT CONGRATULATIONS. DAVID MACLENNAN.

And now, rather tired, I make for bed. The strain of the last fortnight, much as I tried to dissemble it, & cast on stronger shoulders than mine, has been rather hard to bear, and I feel about as weak now as I did when I saw you all again after my adventures abroad last year. Paterson Smyth's chapter on "Responsibility" on page 360 is a noble passage & has helped me this evening.

Goodnight to you all, and dearest love from your affectionate son & brother,

Wilfred Westgate

Trinity College
1.xii.1924

My dear Father,

I do not wish to let Monday pass without a note home: but I have written 11 letters—or cards like this—since Saturday, & cannot do justice to a letter. Many thanks for your congrats: those from home—both you & Mother, & the girls were the most gratifying of all. Everyone in Trinity seemed very glad at my good fortune. Mrs. Bonnycastle sent a delightful letter, too, & this morning's mail brings one from Chester Martin. The request of the Grolier Society seemed rather tasteless: I hope I shall not figure like the old widow in "Punch," whose neighbours were offended at her airs: "Why be Mrs. Flaherty so stuck up these days?" "Och! Since she got her picture in the paper for taking lumbago pills, sure she'll niver speak to a one of us!" I would much rather dismiss them with a polite refusal. Monday morning! It is now 9^{30} and at 10^{10} I have the old fire eater, John MacNaughton.

Love to all,

Bill

P.S. Shield rec'd: thank you for cheque also. Should like a
hamper better than money—chicken, cookies, candy this
term!, i.e. before Dec. 17th.

Trinity College, Toronto
Sunday night [Dec 7, 1924]

Dear Dorothy,

Thank you ever so much for your great letter of congratulations. I got about 25, but those from home were worth the
other two dozen put together.

Last Thursday we had the Annual Athletic Dinner. The
"Saints"—you know by now, I suppose, that these are the girls
of St. Hilda's—send over a cake for every year [class] at
Trinity,—huge, glittering, heavy, majestic cakes about two
feet square and 8 inches thick, inscribed with 2T8, 2T7, 2T6,
and 2T5 in rich ribbons of icing, to designate the various years
'28, '27, '26, and '25. Each year sits at one of 4 long parallel
tables reaching the length of the Great Hall & at the end of
the room, on a dais, sit the dons & speech-makers.

Now it is customary for the Sophomores (2d year) to make
a sally on the 1st year cake, & either carry it off in triumph, or
else wreck it. So when the President of the Athletic Club calls
two 1st year men to the dais to receive the cake, all the worms
rise to guard their two men. The President makes a short
presentation speech & the two worms between them take the
precious cake.

Instantly 2nd year rises, to a man. They fling themselves
on the two worms. But the worms are not undefended: half
their table have rushed up to protect them, and the other half
are on the far side of the table. Suddenly you see a huge
mountain of cake fly into the air! Over the heads of the frantic
Sophomores it soars, & drops into the hands of a worm who
has waited at the table. With cries of indignation, Second year
turns back, & bears down on the 1st year table. But too late!
The man has caught the cake, jumped onto the table, &
clasping it in both arms, is charging down the table, kicking
or crunching underfoot soup plates, apples, ginger ale, cups of

coffee, rolls & butter, and all that usually adorns a banquet
table!

He has almost got to the door, when the gas lights all go
out! He hesitates. He jumps to the floor. He is almost across
the threshold of the Hall, & in safety when, alas! a sophomore
divine, in clerical collar, for he is a deacon, makes a flying
tackle. Phlupp! the cake hits the ground! & its gallant carrier
falls flat on his waistcoat on top of it! One hand is buried to
the wrist in icing & jam sandwich, and in extricating it the
worm rolls over, & digs his other shoulder into the mangled
remains. Immediately three score lunatics are on top of him.
The cake is scattered over the whole floor. Cat-calls of
triumph from Second Year announce that everything is
successfully concluded.

Time would fail to write of the bedlam that reigned
through all the college afterwards. Every corridor was plunged
in darkness. Led by the Head of College, we filed up & down
the whole building with hands on the front man's shoulders,
thumping the floor & bawling songs like maniacs. After
retiring to eat our cakes, & reflect on the success of the
entertainment, we assembled in the hall at 12, and armed
with cornets, flutes, harps, sackbuts, psalteries, & dulcimers,
not to speak of kettles, tongs, blowers, & empty bottles, we
marched over to St. Hilda's & serenaded the celestial
occupants. That done, we came back to bed, & slept till
lunchtime.

Love from Bill

At 14 North View Court   Montreal, P.Q.
390 Côte des Neiges Road   23.xii.1924

My dear Father,

The hour is 9 o'clock on Tuesday morning, and the place
of writing is Dave's room. I have just read a chapter from the
Bible which you and Mother gave to Dave last Convocation:
and quite irresistibly, one's thoughts run back to that day,
and the many, many happy days which Dave and I have spent

together at the University, at St. John's College, and in the
School. Cicero might write his rather shallow essay "De
Amicitia" and observe that "one ought always to treat one's
friends with the consciousness that one day they may be
enemies;" he could count up and compare and balance and
equate, as in an algebraic problem, the advantages of
friendship: but I think it quite obvious that he had no Dave
Mansur in his large circle of acquaintance. The rich financier,
Atticus, was the nearest approximation to a friend: but the
two had not grown up together, and plugged for exams
together, played hockey & tennis & bridge together, been
manacled together in initiations, and thus united, rolled
peanuts along Portage Avenue with their noses, or won the
race back to St. John's from Eaton's on the same eventful
night. Poor old Cicero! His immortal fame for rhetoric and
politics is a tawdry bauble compared to the satisfaction and
delight I felt at seeing Dave in the grey morning at the station
here: for I have tasted enough of fame to know that its
pleasures are ephemeral and unsubstantial: and that the
Kingdom of God is <u>within</u> you.

I will leave for Dorothy's letter the chronicle of my recent
adventures, & tell you what I propose for next term. John
Reade & I are thinking of rooming together in a coffin (ie:
bedroom), but having separate studies. He is only in 1st year,
but he is 21, and of rather nice breeding, though his home life
is sufficiently sad. His father is old and awe-inspiring, his
mother much younger, and wilful, tyrannizing over both
husband and son with the aid of a fictitious weak heart. John
was at school in England, then Brussels, then England again
(an excellent public school called Oundle) and at 16 entered
the Mounted Police, more or less as a runaway from home.
During his childhood at school, the thought of home so
terrified him, & his austere & distant father & his petulant
mother so distressed him, that the prospect of a homecoming
at the end of term would reduce him to tears. He was in the
Mounties for several years, then at a lumber camp, & on an oil
vessel coasting the shores of Chile, and what not. He is

engaged to a girl in Victoria, or Vancouver, & aims to enter
law after he gets his degree in Political Economy, Honours
course. It is quite unusual, of course, for a Graduate to
fraternize with undergrads, and still less with a freshman: but
I think the arrangement will be to our mutual advantage. The
Dean of Residence (Mr. Lloyd Hodgins) smiles on it, so it will
probably materialize—it would be much easier, of course, to
preserve one's dignity by holding aloof from undergrad society,
& living in an Olympian atmosphere which was unapproach-
able by mortals—"on the hills like gods together, careless of
mankind"—but if my dignity is so fragile a thing that it can
only be looked at, & not stand handling, I am content to let it
perish. Provided my work does not follow it.

Frankly, the term is disappointing in retrospect. I appear
to have accomplished little. But perhaps it is not quite
fruitless: I have enjoyed the life of Trinity, & have made the
friendship of several of the professors, & on the whole enjoy
their respect. John MacNaughton still damns me freely, and
screeches in his Bacchanalian frenzy, that I am dreadfully
thick, and appear congenitally incapable of discerning any
intelligent purpose in half the lines of Virgil: but he dismissed
me last Friday with great friendliness, & a jovial warning that
I should not take too great advantage of the superior facilities
for merriment which I would find in the Province of Quebec.
Mr. Owen, brother to the Dean of Hamilton, is the one I like
best. I have been to his house for afternoon tea on Sundays, &
spent a calm, reflective hour over the drawing room fire last
Sunday night. He encouraged me considerably over the past
term's work, & helped me to go home with a much less
despondent feeling.

By the way, do have some of the boys from St. John's out
to a meal now & again. The monotony & hardness of barrack
life in college is horrible, & the influence of an evening in a
quiet refined home, with a mother and girls, is extraordinarily
divine. If I am ever associated with a college or school, or live
near one, & have a nice house, my chief delight will be to have
a family of girls whose influence over the visitors from college

will be half as inspiring as the influence of the one or two nice girls whom I have had the happiness to meet.

I am very sorry not to be home for Christmas. This is the first of four, I suppose, which I must spend in long exile—but it would not be right to wish it otherwise, so I wish you "God rest you, Merry Gentleman" this Christmas Day, and for all the coming year.

Your affectionate son,   R.I. Wilfred Westgate

Suite Quatorze
390 Rue Côte des Neiges
Montreal, P.Q.
25.12.24

Mes chères Soeurs

Voici la lettre que je vous ai promis quand j'ai écris à ma mère. Dans cette ville, tout le monde parle français et anglais, et on voit dans les magasins, et sur les tramways, dans les églises et les proclamations royales, des signes écrites en française et en anglais. J'ai mis à mes amis à Toronto, M. et Mme. Owen, une carte de Nöel française. Mais maintenant, je vais écrire en anglais.

Before I tell you about this ancient city—the largest in Canada—I must send you a word about my doings in Toronto. Well—I enjoyed the reception at S. Hilda's on that eventful Thursday when I wore my dress suit, & the next day invited one Wilma Luxton to come to the Trinity Christmas Dance with me.

This fell on the last Thursday of term. Convocation Hall— the scene of that initiatory ceremony in which the worms did obeisance to the great "Gee Whittaker"—was decorated in black & red, with festoons & curtains, & a fine Christmas tree. The "Saints" all came over under the chaperonage of the saintly Miss Cartwright, & about 8^{15} I took Wilma up to the Hall & had the first two dances with her. The evening sped away as fast as it usually does on such occasions, & it was 1^{30} before I had escorted my partner back to her celestial residence.

I don't think anything that occurred that evening was worthy of particular comment: unless perhaps the fact that on my return from S. Hilda's five or six men dropped into my room and assisted in demolishing the last morsels of those gallant fowl you sent me, & the goodly cake. After they had gone, I lit my fire, & sat down to write an essay, which I was able to hand in at ten next morning.

And now let me say what a royal & princely hamper that was which you sent. I invited Reade & three others to share it with me on the first night: but although 8 of us finally sat upon the case, & did our hungriest, there was still more than half left! It did Reade for about 4 breakfasts—he is constantly over-sleeping in the mornings!—& myself, for surreptitious refreshments at hours from 9 a.m. to 4 a.m., & the dancers on Thursday night,—to say nothing of a family of mice which ate so greedily of it under my bed that, whereas <u>before</u> they had scurried nimbly up & down the wainscoting with only a sort of tickling scrabble, now they paraded along the floor boards with a stately measured tread that shook the building to its foundations! In fact, two or three became intoxicated, & waxed so jovial that I heard their roaring & drinking songs just beside my left ear which faces the wall; & thumping their pewters on the lathes that served for a bar, they would stamp with their scrawny little toes, and clap their sharp little paws, & amid peals of laughter, join in the drinking chorus:

> Three blind wives! Three blind wives!
> Ain't we got fun! Ain't we got fun!
> We'll convulse 'em with tickles, & eat up their pickles
> Until they are pickled, an' won't we be tickled!
> When they're pickled with pickles, an' tickled with tickles,
> Won't-we-have-fun!

On Saturday night there was the Trinity Club dance, after which at 11³⁰ one John Klaehn came into my room as I was undressing: "Westgate, are you on for some fun?" I assured him that at the moment I was bored almost to tears &

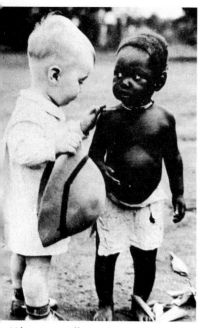

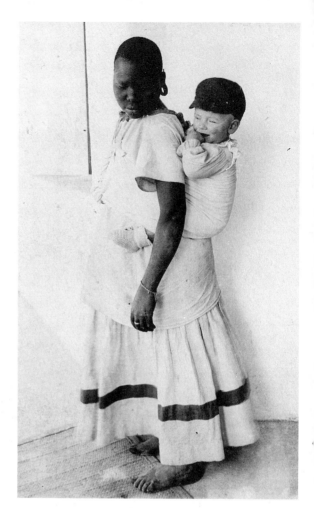

Kiboriani Hills, District of
wapwa, German East Africa where
Westgate was born, September 14,
04. Above: Bill and a friend, circa
06. Right: Bill is carried on the
k of his M'Gogo nurse, "Lutu,"
o is wearing a gown sent from the
cese of Huron in Canada. Below:
ters carry materials from the coast
0 miles to the new mission.

Wilfred, Rita, Dorothy and Maureen in September, 1909, shortly before Rita returned to Afric

...tt Vicarage, where Maureen and
...(right) lived in the care of Reverend
...Mrs. Nightingale from September,
...9 to December, 1912. Below: A
... of the vicarage and its garden,
...h was likened to "a children's
...dise."

Henrietta Georgina Humphrey Malone ("Rita") Westgate's passport photo taken in Novemb[...] 1918 shortly before the family left Ireland for Canada. Right: Thomas Buchanan Reginald ("Rex") Westgate circa 1944.

Below: Moreland Avenue, Croydon, England where the family lived in a rented "rather poke[...] semi-detached" house at number 33 from December, 1912 until war came to London in December, 1915 and they moved to Belfast, Ireland.

rothy, Wilfred and Maureen Westgate's passport photo, November, 1918.

Summer, 1922 on the Sioux Indian Reserve near Griswold, Manitoba, home of descendants the Indians who fled to Canada after the massacre of Custer and his troops at Little Bighorr River in June, 1876. Above: Three "wild young Roman Catholic" Indians pose for Bill. Below A view of the mission taken by Bill with a borrowed wide-angle camera. The church is the building at the far right. In the background is the Assiniboine River with its flooded plain.

bove: Jo Itoye (pronounced "Eataway"), the catechist who preached the service in the Sioux nguage at the mission church below.

Maureen ("Moll") Westgate and a friend (name unknown) circa 1925.

Below: The wreck of the cattle train, May 31, 1923, on its way to Montre[al] "A great boulder, the size of the kitch[en] table," rolled on to the tracks. The engineer jammed on the brakes, but could not stop. The engine "by its ow[n] momentum was levered off the rails, carried over the stone and deposited [on] the roadbed."

arritz, France with the McKaigs.
left to right are Jim McKaig, age
Mrs. McKaig (in white); Miss
rude Sands; Clem McKaig, age
and Bill Westgate.

w: Bill astride his motorbike
octetes."

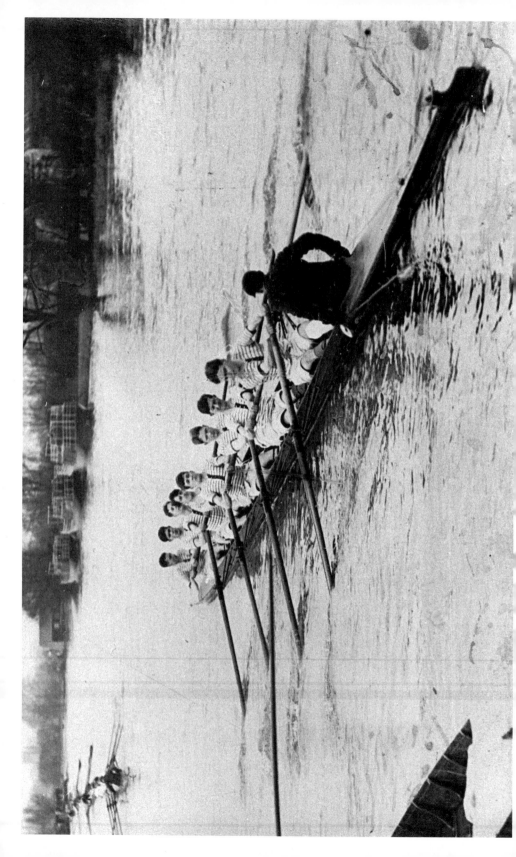

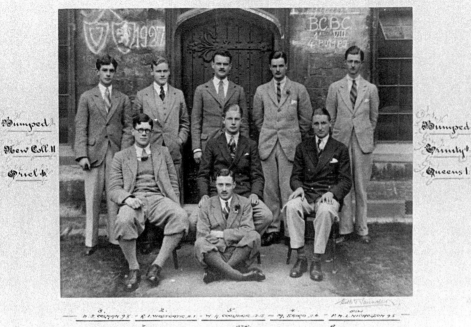

cing page: Balliol II Toggers Week, February, 1927. Bill Westgate is stroke (next to the cox in rk jacket). The team made three bumps, ending 7th in the first division, higher than any cond Togger had ever been before. According to a list Bill wrote on a celebration dinner enu, the members of the team, from stern to bow, are: H. J. Pelham (cox); R.I.W. Westgate ; P. N. L. Nicholson (7); W. A. Ebbert (6); J. S. Sommers- Cox (5); P. J. Thompson (4); A. D. Peterson (3); Hon. E. J. Stanley (2); and G. H. S. Du Ponte (1). Substitutes were R. H. atthias on Tuesdays and Hon. C. E. Freemantle on Wednesdays and Thursdays.

ove: Balliol College 1st Eight, May, 1927. The list of bumps are: New College, II; Oriel, I; nity, I; and Queens, I. The men are top row left to right: D. S. Colman (3); R. I . W. estgate (2); W. A. Coolidge (5); M. Baird (4); and R. N. Nicholson (bow). Second row, ated: D. J. V. Bevan (7); W. S. LLewellyn (stroke); and T. R. Peppercorn (6). Front on the ound: R. H. Mathias (cox).

Bill Westgate at the time of his *Literae Humaniores*, or "Greats," examinatio for his B.A. in Classics at Oxford in June, 1930. Note the small mascot d on his knee.

Below: "Going across" in 1928. The men are, left to right, Andrew Lang, David Bevan, Matt Baird, Alfred Mitchell, Trevor Peppercorn, Hugh Pryce, Mason Hamond, Hon. Edward Stanley and Robinson on the pole.

The marriage of Bill Westgate and Sheila Margaret Dann, July 11, 1934 at St. Chad's Church, Shrewsbury, England.

Phillips Academy, Andover, Massachusetts where Bill taught Latin and Ancient History from 1935 to 1944. Above: Not all pyramids are on the Nile! Bill is standing on the left and Shei Westgate is peering over the top of the pile in Adams Hall.

Below: Bill in his classroom in Pearson Hall, Andover. The wall posters, given by Bill, are still there.

ve: Sheila and Bill enjoy a St. Bernard's Sports Day outing.

w: A Westgate family portrait taken in the fall of 1949 in their living room at St. Bernard's. to right are Margaret E. Dann, Sheila's mother; Bill; Brig. Gen. W. R. H. Dann, Sheila's er; Michael Westgate; Sheila; Diana Westgate and "Flippy."

Bill "at home" in Chatham, Massachusetts where he spent his last years active and contente until his death in July, 1988.

would welcome even such relief as his meager intelligence could afford. "Well, we'll go down to the dance hall, slip in unobserved, turn off the gas which lights the place, swipe the handle, & beat it! Let's go, Reade, & do it now!"

At first I refused to spoil a private party like that, but when we arranged that we shd. return the handle within five minutes, & do the thing humorously, I agreed. Our line of retreat was through a dining-room window & up the fire escape: and we were in perfect readiness when the orchestra struck up "Good Night, Ladies"—& our chance was gone. However, we found a few odd plates of ice cream, & took them to the dining-room: where, finding that only one table was laid, and that the don's table, we used it. Reade sat in the Dean's chair, Klaehn in the Provost's, & I in the Registrar's. Afterwards, we collected all the salt-cellars & tipped them into the sugar basin while we filled the salt shakers with sugar: &, leaving all in perfect order, retired to bed. We slept in the common room that night & Sunday night—bringing our sheets & pillows & blankets down & spreading them on the sofas, etc. which had been left there from the dance. The gyp [servant] made up the fire from time to time, & we were thoroughly comfortable.

I caught an 11 o'c train from Toronto on Monday night, & after a tiresome journey, was met at 7^{30} by Dave on Tuesday morning. Today Dave & I were to have gone to 8 o'c service at Christ Church, but overslept—Heavens! how weary I have been! What a relaxation to get away from Trinity's barrack life! to old friends, & a lovely house, & a most glorious old city!—However, I went down at 9^{15} & saw the Dean. Instead of going to the 9^{30} service, I returned for breakfast; & before I noticed it, the time was 11.

I am very sorry, indeed, to have let Christmas pass without actually attending divine service: it seems barren, dull, worldly, and so drab. The angels, and the shepherd's vision, the manger & Holy Mother, the pilgrim sages, the Holy Innocents, and the glory of the Eternal Father—all these beauties are shut out, & one is left with a hollow celebration of a meaningless tradition, unless one is shown into the mysteries which the Church of God alone reveals. How would I willingly exchange our jolly merry-making here—a most sumptuous dinner at Dave's aunt's, with an elephant metamorphosed into a turkey for the first course, & a rich plum pudding for the second, &, after a drive with Peggy & Dave, cake & a glass of ancient port—how would I jump to exchange it all for a simple day at home: early communion at St. Luke's, breakfast, that noble service in the dear old church at 11, then presents, & dinner, & a walk with Hasted, or an afternoon with the Careys, & an evening for reading!

I am writing now at Dave's home, at 6 or 7 o'c., and in an hour or so must prepare for a show at the "Princess." When we were driving, we bought a Monday *Free Press*. How jolly to see the old rag again! Perhaps I asked you before, but whether or no, <u>please</u> do not fail to send one copy of the *Free Press* (or *Tribune*), when the results of the Christmas exams are issued, to Dave, & one to me.

<u>P-l-e-a-s-e</u>, do not forget it!

I can assure you that at times I envy Dave. He is now out in the world earning an independent living of $100 per month, & generous bonuses. And his mother & sister are most happily settled. I, on the contrary, cannot hope to earn one copper for three & a half years: I must draw from, & contribute nothing, all the time from Father's funds: & they, I know, are hardly enough to keep you in ordinary comfort. What a palace I will lodge you all in when I first draw salary! We shall live in Montreal—what a drab old village that Winnipeg is!—& live simply as hermits, but have nice friends to stay with us, & a small car, or three horses, & skis, & a cutter, & a good big den for the Pater, with a roaring log in its ample hearth, & a holly bush outside the mullioned window! Hurray! Just 6 Christmases from today, we shall have it! So cheer up, & have a jolly old Christmas, & smite the turkey hip & thigh, & usher in the Merry New Year with a flowing bowl of Johnnie Walker, & the strident blare of "der Doppel Adler."

From your half-wit brother,   Bill

Trinity College
Jan. 4, 1925

My dearest Mother

I wish you many happy returns of the day, and add the hope that I may be present with you for most of those many returns. For a birthday present, I spent most of the morning trying to compose a sonnet to you: but the versification of a sonnet is the most difficult of all English types of poetry, and takes days & days to polish up: the rhymes are not perfect in this, and the metre rather shaky, but I'll send it as it is now, & perhaps do it better another day. But I'll ask you, please when you have read it, to burn it: you can keep the finished edition that I hope is to follow.

Thank you ever so much for your book: at present I am reading Samuel Butler's *The Way of All Flesh*, but the next will be *The High Way*.

My New Year has started well with a good dash of work, & promises to be very happy in the immediate future, and not less so in the year's decline. I might repeat here the warning that I may have to forego the Toronto M.A., because my first consideration is not a Toronto M.A., but preparation for Oxford: however, I still hope for the best.

Now Goodnight, dear Mother. I hope before the year is very old I may see you all again. Father I expect in February.

With dearest love & kindest wishes. Your son,

Wilfred W.

Trinity College
Toronto, Ontario
Sunday afternoon, 11.i.25

Dear Dorothy,

It seems ages since I addressed a letter to you, so this note will bear the insignificant title of Dorothy Westgate: please let me hear from you in reply as soon as possible.

What you will have to reply to I do not know, for I cannot think what to write: however, I have no doubt it will be a very runcible letter when it is finished, and so I'll begin it.

Dear Dorothy: One of the second year men,—Cameron Crosthwait, an old T.C.S.[1] or Port Hope boy,—brought a little girl to Trinity, last Monday I think. She was about eleven, and Helen was her name-O. Few of the students had then returned, so Cam and Helen and I had afternoon tea in the tea-room-O. She was very shy, and hardly said a word, and when I tactlessly proposed that she should pour out the tea, she twiddled her fingers so much that it made me giddy-O, (which rhymes, you know, with *video*!) Well, when Helen went away about an hour later, Cam saw her home, and then bought a book for her. It was verses by Edward Lear, who was a melancholy old person in ordinary life, but wrote screamingly funny nonsense verses for children. He says of himself, in his absurd autobiography:

He has many friends laymen and clerical,
Old Foss is the name of his cat,
His body is perfectly spherical,
He weareth a runcible hat.

You don't know what runcible means? Well, that's the whole story. John Reade was in my room when Cam came back, and read this silly stuff, and of course we found it all very funny, though none of us knew what runcible meant. At last we came to a line about my Aunt Jublisca's runcible spoon! Ha! now we could find out what runcible meant! we would write to Ryrie-Birks [a jewelry store] for quotations on "one runcible spoon, solid silver, suitable for a wedding present," and see what they would reply! And this we did.

Next morning, I was called out of my bath to answer a telephone call, and when I picked up the receiver, a melancholy voice enquired, "Mr Westgate? This is Ryrie-Birks speaking, Mr. Westgate! (My heart sank into my bedroom slippers) You sent us an order yesterday, Mr Westgate, for one r-r-r-r-rrruncible spoon."

"Y-y-y-yyyessss," I replied, with chattering teeth, "I did."

"Now could you, Mr Westgate, tell us what sort, exactly ---
- er, we have looked through all our catalogues, and - er - the
managers of the various departments have been consulted,
but we cannot find exactly a runcible spoon."

"Oh," I replied, "that's funny. It's for a wedding present,
you know!"

"Yes, Mr Westgate, but could you, --- try if you could
describe it exactly, --- we are not quite sure what sort of spoon
a runcible spoon is!"

Well, by this time, of course, I was splitting, and had to
put the old codger off with a promise to enquire more
precisely of a friend of mine, whom, I explained, I had
volunteered to assist by making enquiries. So that's that.

The afternoon tea bell has gone, and I must go down to
the common room. At seven, I am going to see Monsieur
Bisson, the French lecturer, to ask him about arrangements
for spending the summer in France. I'll finish this letter later.

With love to all from your affectionate brother,

Bill

[1] Trinity College School

Trinity College
Toronto
Wed, 2^{pm} Jan 22nd 1925

My dear Father,

As my Sunday correspondence did not expand beyond the
limits of a card, and as I feel quite cheerful at the moment, I
will fill this sheet with my news and views.

I have a major part in a minor play which is to be staged
at Hart House on Feb. 6th & 7th. The Trin. Coll. Dramatic Soc.
are acting Bernard Shaw's "Androcles & the Lion" wh. deals
with early Christian persecutions, & the curtain-raiser is a
humorous skit, "The Man in the Bowler Hat" by A.A. Milne. I
portray that character for wh. Nature & art have conspired to
equip me, The Chief Villain, of the really low-brow, heavy-
jawed, drinking, swearing, cudgelling type. The experience is

valuable to me, & as the piece is very short, I do not lose much time at rehearsals or at the final presentations.

Financially I flourish. My cheque for $167^{00} came in last week, & I have repaid you $70^{00}, thus docking your Jan. salary $30^{00}. A non-paying pupil has come to me already—he is due for some Virgil in 10 minutes, & will attract others.

John MacNaughton has set me a most interesting essay on Eschatology[1] of Virgil, & when I read him the first part this morning, seemed pleased. And old Maurice Hutton told me my Greek prose was vastly better & showed good promise, while a Latin one got A^{+} last Monday. This is most encouraging to me, & I think it will be to you.

—Oh, I must tell you about a hockey game I refereed on Monday between Ontario Agricultural College & Trinity. I have lost my skates, you know, & so had to borrow a pair, which fitted me like horse-troughs, & I had to spend such care & energy on keeping myself upright, that half the foul plays got by, & the game became very ragged. Once, indeed, skating backwards, my feet stuck, & describing a scholarly parabola, I landed with a sudden phlump! on my shoulders. In the last 2 mins. I put 4 men off for foul play, & then in the universal uproar I did not hear the time keeper's whistles! & let the play proceed for 15 seconds till Trinity scored a goal! Finally I had to get both managers to taxi up to Hart House & explain everything to the committee. The result is quite happy.

Here is my "coachee," so I must stop. With dearest love to Mother & the girls, your affectionate son,

W.W.

---

[1] Eschatology: The branch of religion dealing with the four last things: death, judgement, heaven and hell.

Trinity College
Sunday afternoon,
8.ii.25

My dear Mother,

...I am content to work like a Trojan at Latin & Greek till
Easter, (or rather the end of term, about May 15th) till I feel at
home in that field of literature, history, philosophy, art &
science: then have a glorious burst of reading in English—
Shaw, Wordsworth, Shakespeare, Dickens, Scott & Thackeray:
besides the moderns, like Milne & Masefield & Butler & Hardy
& Barrie. Finally, to have a good holiday in France & learn the
language & customs & conversation & literature & politics &
government there.—As to the summer, I do not yet know what
we can do. Dr. Orchard, the head of Trinity College School
(Port Hope) cannot promise me a mastership there for the
summer term, but will put my name on his files. I will now
write to Upper Canada & Ridley. But I _do_ want to spend some
time in France before October, when I must go to Balliol.
...Whatever happens to us, you at all events must go to
England & Ireland _this_ summer.

Love from Bill

Trinity College
15.iii.1925

My dearest Pater

Instead of going to chapel at 11 this morning, I stayed in
my room and read MacLear on Confirmation. The more I dip
into the prayer book and see the history of the Church, the
more impressed and awed I am with its historic grandeur, and
its tradition of noble piety and devotion. To glance down the
catalogue of saints and martyrs in the calendar; to read the
Collects, in the light of their authors' circumstances, and feel
the anguish in one, the calm repose of well-grounded
confidence in another, the yearning for holiness in a third, the
majestic ascription of glory and honour and might and power
in a fourth: to feel the regal pomp and circumstance in some
of its processional hymns, and the sweet consolation breathed

in its devotional hymns, and the slow and awe-full calmness of the brooding presence of God in some communion hymns (especially, I think, in "God reveals His presence")—all this stirs in one a patriotic pride, and devotion, and love that nothing, I hope, can ever shake in us. But it does not necessarily breathe religion, or even honest morality.

I mean that often the Church is just a great idol, which we worship most devotedly; which is a fine institution; which lifts our life above the ordinary smallnesses of the day. But it is no more than Athens was to the Athenians, or La France was to the armies of Napoleon.

I remember that Pericles, when he pronounced the funeral oration over the heroes of Athens who fell in the first year of the war with Sparta, spoke thus "And to you who remain, I would say but this: Think on the greatness of your city night and day; cast your eyes upon her beauty and splendor, and let them sink deep within your soul till you conceive a passion for her, and become, as it were, her lovers, and are filled with devotion for her." So also the Church is a monument of greatness: finer by far than even the "School of Hellas" whom her poets celebrate thus:

O rich and renowned, and with violets crowned,
O Athens! the envied of nations!

But to me there seems much that is superstitious and bigoted; not free and open, but hidebound and tabu; not intelligent, but theological. Aesthetically speaking, superb; but philosophically unnecessary and undesirable. I frequently wish we lived a simple, pastoral life (you see I have been reading Virgil's *Bucolics*!) where our whole duty was to do justly, to love mercy, and to walk humbly with our God.

Don't, please, think me to be floundering in the morasses of theory, after a mere will-o-the-wisp. I feel myself awakening from a horrible sort of torpor of indifference, or lethargy & apathy which hung all about me through the winter: doubts are beginning to rise again and grow more & more insistent, and spur me out of the unhealthy and unnatural apathy of the last 4 months.

On Fri. I had aft. tea with Mr. Grant, the head of Upper Canada College School (a Balliol "first" himself, in classics). I met 2 other masters, one an ex-Rhodes man, one a history man from Balliol. The latter, Grier, took me over the School, & then to dinner. How I should love to go there as a master!

Ever your affectionate son,

Wilfred.

Trinity College
29.iii.1925

My dearest Mother

This is the time when I write my best letters home to you, namely Sunday mornings, when everyone else is in chapel. So, although I am up only half an hour, and want to read for an hour before lunch, I will try to cover this page.

First, what of the summer? If I get my M.A.—which I greatly doubt—I should have to stay here till June 6th or so, (& perhaps be back for Dorothy's birthday.) If I got a lucrative job in Winnipeg, & could make say \$200^{00} by September, it might be best to spend the summer with you. But even with my M.A., I shall not be half so well prepared for Oxford as the V & VI form boys from Winchester & elsewhere: so that I am most eager to get some good coaching, from a man like Laurie, or else from a French tutor near Paris, before I go up to Balliol in October. As for finances, the position is this: my fellowship here will not settle my Trinity accounts, by some \$100^{00}. This sum, (as I said last week) I will take the responsibility for; if I can't pay it off at once, I'll make terms with the college for it.

Now, the summer in France or England or Ireland would cost approx. 1000 francs per month, ie: \$55^{00}. At that, I could cross the Atlantic in a cattle boat again, & so save a couple of hundred. The question is, therefore, will there be enough funds in the family coffers, after you & Moll have purchased tickets for England & made the other necessary outlays, and after provision has been made for a holiday of some sort for Dorothy & the Pater, to let me spend $150^{00} to $200^{00} on living in France?

Taking Father's current income only into consideration, the scheme is impossible. And it is equally unthinkable to sell out invested capital. But if there is a sum coming to me by inheritance, I think this would be the most advantageous way to employ it, because the advantage of going up to Balliol with a good polish in Latin & Greek, and two months' acquaintance with French as a spoken tongue, plus the general savoir-faire that a short time on the continent is calculated to give one, would be invaluable, I shd. think, to start with.

To revert to selling investments—I don't see why I should not sell my war bonds & so realize at least $100^{00}. On 100 I could do something in France: you see, I'd go to England by cattle boat for nothing, then to France for a few shillings, and hunt up a tutorial bureau in Paris. There I would meet an Alsatian count of boundless wealth & unlimited generosity, seeking for a Toronto M.A. of one or two & twenty, who would be willing to coach his young son in tennis, & swimming, & golf, & riding, & instruct him in Latin, Greek & English.

In return for this, his only daughter, a princess of the Bourbon blood, of some nineteen summers, would like to teach me drawing & music, take me driving through the Vosges, and forest of Ardennes, and plan a trip down the Rhine Valley. I shall write to you then of my movements, but you had better address my mail: poste restante, % M. le Conte de Bien-Riche, le Palais d'Or, Alsace! I should be quite content to go afoot to Paris, & take the chance of finding some such position: if I failed, I should still have my $100^{00} and when that was exhausted, could return to England and live with Hubert till term began.

However, all this apart, I am most anxious to return to Winnipeg before I go to Balliol, & also, if possible, to see the Rockies. Reade & I were speaking of their wonders last night.

I am quite resolved on this point.—& I'm sure Father is too—that you & Moll MUST go over to England this year. Moll,

I think, should go with the Overseas Education League: & I think that you could go on the same boat, even if you could not occupy the same quarters that are reserved for the undergrads.

One very remarkable event occurred this week—the "Valedictory" last Friday. After a meeting of the Lit., refreshments were served in Hall at 9^{30}. Valedictory speeches were made by all the departing members, including myself, and the evening went rather tediously away till 11^{30}. Then four former Scribes of the Venerable Father Episcopôn entered the hall. The present scribe read to all the assembled college, a most impressive charge to carry on the traditions of old Trinity to the new Trinity in Queen's Park. Then there was a lockstep round the building, till we finally lined up on the terrace in front of the college. In dead silence we stood, gathered on the lawn, while the bell in the lantern tower tolled 28 (for the year 2T8). Then a taper light appeared in the tower, and waved to and fro in a ghostly fashion. Another minute & a big lantern was lighted up there, and shed its soft and mellow light abroad. Now a quaint, old-fashioned coach drove up to the door. The light in the high tower was extinguished, and again we waited in hushed expectancy.

One, two, three minutes must have gone, before the great door opened. Two dim figures, bearing torches, came forth— former scribes of Episcopôn. Then another; and, leaning on this scribe's arm, a figure, bent with years, white with the snows of upwards of fourscore winters, and bearing an antique staff. Two other scribes—one the present Head of College, one the present Provost,—bearing their flaring links, followed the Venerable Father, and then the doors of old Trinity closed, and for ever, upon Father Episcopôn. This slow procession of flamens broke into a solemn chant as they brought him to the waiting carriage: a chant was lifted up by all who stood about. He entered the vehicle, with the present scribe and the scribe of 2T4. Nor did the chant die away till the yellow flare of the torches became a pin point of light vanishing & again appearing through the trees as the carriage drove across the park. It was a spectacle that I hope will prove indelible in my mind. It was magnificent. Would that St. John's had such traditions!

By now it was all but 12, and a wing fight was proposed. Eastern Wing vs. Western. Half an hour was granted to barricade the W. Wing, & to let the combatants arm: then a most bloody conflict ensued. Pails of water were sluiced broadcast: garments and faces rent from top to bottom & from ear to ear, and all the unfortunate captives were plunged willy-nilly into a brimming bath. Tom Taylor, Caesar de Lour, Catchpole, & I tried to force a secret passage by the servants' quarters, the "Gooseneck," but without effect.

At 12^{30} we serenaded St. Hilda's with songs & howls & pokers on pails. Then we lit a hugh bonfire, which brought round two fire reels. After a ride of a hundred yards on a fire reel (for they very soon turned homeward again), we had to pile off, because the engine had got stuck in mud. By now the fire was dying: we put it out, & congregated in small knots in different rooms. Taylor & I were for going downtown to Bowles for something to eat: Bissett & Charleson (you remember that I spent the day at Ottawa with Charleson) joined us, & Escott Reid & Cam Crosthwait. I could not describe all our garments: for my part, I had underwear (badly ripped from rugby at the knee), hockey pants, sweater, Moll's pajama pants, dressing gown, running shoes, a dirty old hat, & a scarlet Trinity blazer. After refreshment at Bowles, we ascended the steps of the City Hall, and Bissett delivered a magnificent oration, on what he can't remember; and as everyone else was also making speeches, nobody can tell him just what his theme was. He was dressed, I recall, as a bishop of the Greek Orthodox Church—except that for stole & hood, he had a window curtain tied round his neck: this stays in my memory because I did the knotting, and almost got wounded on the curtain pins & rings which were still in it. About 2^{45} we boarded a street car & stumbled home about 3: at that hour, five of us began to argue on the spelling of "supersede," but when two fell asleep, the remainder found to their dismay that they were all arguing on the same side, and, to prevent serious results, at once went to bed. To this hour, I'm still as hoarse as a crow.

I must see Cosgrave again soon. He is my best friend here, quite.

Love, Bill

— IX —
"I HOPED TO BE A GREAT HEADMASTER"
(June—August, 1925)

Trinity College
Toronto, Ontario
June 2nd, 1925

Cyril Bailey, Esq.
Balliol College
Oxford.

Dear Mr. Bailey:

I am afraid that you will consider as unsatisfactory the amount of work that I have done this year at the University of Toronto. I have read all Virgil, but not all carefully; the first four books of Tacitus's *Annals*, in the same way; and (instead of the trilogy of Aeschylus which I proposed to you last autumn) I have done six plays of Euripides. I have also read, more carefully, the Poetics of Aristotle and of Horace. This, with Greek and Latin compositions, and five or six English essays, composes my work for the year.

If there be reasons to seek, the chief one, I think, is that I have worked almost entirely without supervision. The experience may be good for one, but I am glad that I do not have to continue it much longer.

I hope to sail for England in mid-July, and then to spend August and September in France. I am expecting to go up for Honour Mods. in 1926, and for that reason I shall try to secure a tutor for the summer in France. Meanwhile, I shall continue to grind savagely at Cicero and Demosthenes in the hope of catching something of their style. I should be very glad to see you in July, if you happened to be in Oxford then, to get from you some last words of advice before the Michaelmas term; I have, however, a copy of the Statutes for Mods., as well as a "Notice" which Mr. Pickard-Cambridge sent to me last summer, so that from these I can easily arrange what I ought to read with a tutor.

The most convenient address one can give for correspondence after the 15th of July is "% Dr. A.H. Watson, 35 Castle Road, Salisbury, Wilts." If it is the thing to do, I should like to speak for a room in College now, but it is my impression, however, that the end of July will not be too late to do this. Would you therefore have the necessary papers and forms sent to me at Salisbury, if you please?

I am, Yours sincerely, W.W.

AUTOBIOGRAPHY

[I had] a poor year as a graduate student with a graduate scholarship in Classics, living in the old Trinity College in Toronto. In the decaying old building, far distant from the University, there was little to engage a young graduate like myself in corporate life. I should have joined the choir. I joined the Drama Club and made a few friends that way playing in "The Man With the Bowler Hat," but I had little in common with live undergraduates and knew no one in Toronto till the Rev. F.H. Cosgrave invited me to his parish for Sunday service at St. Clement's and supper at his house with a reading of poetry...

The then Dean of the College showed little interest in counselling students, and I felt often miserably "out of it," making friends very slowly...I was clearly too immature for the student world of eastern Canada, unless it provided good counselling, so my tutorial course in Virgil proved merely eccentric, my course in Greek Composition very advanced, and a tutorial course in Euripides above my head. I did not pass all my examinations and did not emerge with a Toronto M.A., nor was I much helped toward success when I should eventually enter Balliol.

I blame myself for rushing into a graduate year of work in circumstances for which I was not ready, and deeply regret the lack of guidance received either at home or in Manitoba or in Toronto. In truth, I did not know how to seek [guidance], and ended my Toronto year rather shrunken than expanded.

SMW

Bill carried out his wish to see the Rockies by working in the kitchen of a Pullman train to Vancouver and back to Winnipeg, where he arrived home on June 15th. There he spent most of the next two months reading the classics in preparation for Balliol, and earned some money hay-making at Griswold. His mother, with Dorothy and Moll, left Winnipeg on June 23rd and landed at Glasgow July 7th, 1925. Bill set out for England via cattle train, visiting friends in Toronto and Port Hope before boarding the S.S. *Gracia* at Montreal as a cattleman on August 15th. Here he received a letter from his father:

513 McMillan Ave.
Winnipeg
Saturday, Aug. 8th, 1925

My very dear Wilfred,

I am going to send you a brief message of cheer to meet you at Montreal, to wish you good luck in the Name of the Lord, and to say that you will be faithfully remembered in prayer day by day. I have missed you dreadfully all day, but thank God for a full day of toil which has kept me from dwelling more than I otherwise should on the thought of our separation for three years...

I have had a hard time keeping a straight face today. Tears want to come. Truly great is a Father's love for his children. I understand something of what God's love meant for the world when He gave His only son. You will not find any-where a better Friend than Christ. He is so companionable also. Make him your confidante. He has more wisdom than Plato, and He is utterly unselfish. Write me freely. I will help you with all my might. You have brought great credit to us

all, and we are all justly proud of you. You will continue to do
this for us at Oxford.

Ever, dear Bill, your most devoted father,

Thomas B. R. Westgate

S.S. *Gracia* (Donaldson Line)
in the St. Lawrence
Friday night [August 14, 1925]

My dearest Pater

You cannot imagine my delight when the steward, who
was signing me in at the docks this morning, said to me
"Westgate? I got some mail for you on board. You can get it in
ten minutes." It was most encouraging to get your message: if
I have brought honour to the family, it is but a shallow and
popular type of honour which is very different from the more
quiet but much more sterling, much more lustrous, much
more serene honour, that those who know you ascribe to you.

Dave was not less delighted than surprised to see me: and
together we had a glorious 2 days (Wed. & Thurs.). We saw
Australia beat Canada in the Davis Cup (World's Amateur
Championship) preliminaries at Mt. Royal tennis courts
yesterday. We got up today at 6^{am}, had breakfast at the house,
& then taxied to the docks to shed 5. The *Gracia* is a ghastly
hulk!

Perhaps when you were my age you had a friend who
would do absolutely anything for you at any cost, & all with a
grace that was innocent of all interested motives beyond the
pleasure of helping you. If you hadn't, you can but faintly
picture what Dave has meant for me. When I was dressing
this morning, he brought me a magnificent pair of German
binoculars which his father commandeered overseas: knowing
what D. thought of his father, I could hardly help being moved
when he said that I was to keep them while I was abroad. He
saw me off at shed 5 at 8 o'c.

[Further pages, if any, are missing]

7 Buckleigh Road, Streatham
Tuesday evening, 25.viii.25

My dearest Pater

My letter from the pilot-place at Quebec gave you an idea
of how pleasant a journey I had to Montreal, and how
pleasant a stay with the Shearers. To steam down the lordly
St. Lawrence must kindle some flame of patriotic pride and
exultation in any man, and at the same time give him a sense
of calm serenity that breeds a confident strength. If you'd like
to read "The Last Chantey" by Kipling, you will find it in a
little red volume of poetry in my room, called *Shakespeare to
Hardy*: it's only about fifty lines long.

St. John (as we may for convenience call him), you
remember, writes that God, at the end of time, shall take
away the sea: this decision (in "The Last Chantey") is at the
last moment revised, for there is so much of mercy and
compassion and courage and open-heartedness associated with
the sea that to gather it up for the final day of destruction
would be to annihilate those virtues. Therefore—

Wind, hail, and rain shall not fail from the face of it,
Stinging, ringing spindrift, and the fulmar flying free,
    That they who have no pleasure
    For to serve the Lord by measure
May enter into galleons and serve Him on the sea.[1]

There are some lovely lines in the ballad: the reproachful
words of "Judas that betrayed Him," and the pitiful tribute to
the mercy of God, from "the souls of the slaves that men
threw overboard;" the reckless bravado of the gentlemen-
adventurers, "Fettered wrist to bar all for red iniquity," and,
at last, the hasty and impetuous exclamation of the chorus of
the jolly, jolly mariners, who are chagrined at the boredom of
the heavenly drawing-room—

    Must we sing for evermore
    On this windless, glassy floor?

Take back your golden fiddles, and we'll beat to open sea!

These all breathe of an open, healthy, vigorous theology that the conventional Churchman is sometimes apt to ignore. Personally, I was affected by certain sights on the St. Lawrence, and in the midnight sky when I slept for two nights on deck, in much the same way as I was when we knelt about Aunt Kathleen's bed after breakfast this morning for prayers.

I am sorry to preach in my letters:—but, of course, I have unimpeachable precedent for epistolary homilies! Our passage was smooth even in mid-Atlantic, and was completed in ten days and some five hours.

Ireland was sighted on Sunday morning. Rathlin Island, & the Giant's Causeway, Larne, Belfast, all passed in rapid succession that afternoon & evening: about 11 o'c (after Molesworth & I had eaten almost a loaf of bread which we toasted in the galley) we climbed the mainmast & from that height caught sight of a light from the Isle of Man. I was too excited to go to bed before 1^{00} & sat for'ard talking to the lookout: I was naturally sleepy when we got up at 3^{30} in the morning to do the rounds of the decks, but a very idle Monday, spent or misspent chiefly in missing tides and missing our turns at the dock, allowed me plenty of leisure to doze and rest. When we got ashore at 6 p.m. at Liverpool, Molesworth and I had tea downtown with the vet before I saw the former off to Ireland at the Dublin Dock.

At midnight I met Frank, and together we travelled to Euston. From there by various stages I travelled to Streatham, and (as I said before) this morning at 8 o'c reached Aunt Kathleen's and had breakfast with Walter.—I do not think that I shall ever love any book as I shall love Job. On the *Gracia* I read & reread the chapter on wisdom, and this evening I cannot help picking it up again, and dreaming of it till again I sit on the side of your bed, and as I listen to the evening breezes stir in the maples, hear your voice saying

"Behold, the fear of the Lord, that is wisdom, and to depart from Evil is understanding."

With very dear love from   **Bill**

[1] Bill's recollection of the Kipling poem was somewhat confused. The last two stanzas are:

Then stooped the Lord, and He called the good sea up to Him,
    And 'stablished its borders unto all eternity,
        That such as have no pleasure
        For to praise the Lord by measure,
    They may enter into galleons and serve Him on the sea.

Sun, Wind, and Cloud shall fail not from the face of it,
    Stinging, ringing spindrift, nor the fulmar flying free;
        And the ships shall go abroad
        To the Glory of the Lord
    Who heard the silly sailor-folk and gave them back their sea!

[From *Modern American & British Poetry* edited by James Untermeyer, New York, N.Y. Harcourt Brace & Co., 1930.]

Mother   112 rue Montmartre
LISEZ ET AVANCEZ   Paris, Tue. 6^{30}a.m.
S.V.P.   8.9.1925

My dearest Father,

    Aeons of ages have passed since I saw you: in measure of time it is only a month, in the measure of memory it is a thousand ages. Here am I, at half past six in the morning, writing from my bed in a little hotel in Paris, to give you an account of the last few weeks,—and, parbleu! I feel as if I were embarking upon a history of the world!

    To be brief—Sat. at night I crossed on a cheap excursion (33f. return London-Paris!), reached Paris Sunday at 7 a.m., slept in this hotel till 4 p.m., had a splendid walk in the afternoon and evening, and after a deep sleep again, called on Monday morning on Mr. Stanley Hidden.

It would be a long story to describe my difficulties in finding him—difficulties due to the fact that there are 2 rues St. Honoré! but when I got there, I had only said a few words when Hidden,—a young Englishman—said "You wouldn't like a tutoring post, would you, for yourself, and be paid for it? An American lady is going to Biarritz—a most fashionable watering place near the Pyrénées—at once: she is extremely nice, and well-to-do, and wants someone to look after her 2 boys, 11 & 9, and give them tennis & swimming, etc. for the next 2-3 weeks. We find it impossible, at this time of year, to suit her. If you like it, please call at 6 or 7 this evening."

I called, and after I had seen Mrs. McKaig, decided to go with her & them to Biarritz tomorrow (Wed. the 9th).

At 1 today I'm to have lunch with the McKaigs at the Hotel Cambon, in the American quarter of the city. My engagement really commences from this afternoon, therefore, when the boys & I are to go out together somewhere. Do not you think that all these events are strong indications that there _is_ a divinity that shapes our plans, rough-hew them how we will? I was distressed with the loneliness of this strange city, and now I am given 2 rather jolly youngsters to go about with, & the chance of reading & tennis & a holiday at a quiet "pension" near one of the loveliest spots of Europe: for Mrs. McK. will not have a dressy hotel. We are managing very well, I think, in England & France.

I do hope that you are faithfully doing your best to keep strong and comfortable on your side of the water. If anything happened to you, the joys which we have enjoyed, and are promised for the next 3 or 4 months over here, would become as bitter and galling as now they are pleasant. If you can stand the hardship of being alone for this length of time, I believe you will be rewarded when you see Mother looking so much better, and Moll improved in French and otherwise after a long and happy holiday. Dorothy I have not seen since we both saw her in Winnipeg, but I promise myself a visit to Brighton on my return to England.

With very dear love from your affectionate son, Bill

P.S. Except with you, I compel myself to correspond in French. I wonder if Mother derives from my letters the meaning which I intend to convey!

Villa Arnould   Sunday afternoon
Place de l'Atalaye   27.ix.1925
Biarritz

My dear Pater

Our holiday at Biarritz is lacking but half a day of its end. Jim, who shares my room, is busy packing—with all the boredom and dawdliness that a boy of 12 commonly feels toward such an old maid's occupation. As for me, my clothes are packed, and in readiness for the family chariot which tomorrow morning will take us to the "Gare du Midi" and the train for Paris. After a day in Paris my engagement—thank God!—is up, and I catch the first boat-train to the Channel, to Dorothy, to London, and Balliol.

Do not think that my gratitude for the termination of my tutorship is evoked by the unpleasantness of my duties. Far from it. I have enjoyed almost every moment of the past three weeks. I shall look back on them with the liveliest delight, and shall keep an eye on Jim & Clem, but especially Jim, as long as my eyes can follow them. And as for Mrs. McKaig, she has proved charming. "It will be time enough"—one might say, "to pronounce her charming when she has given you her financial farewell."

Perish the thought! My holiday has cost me nothing: I have had abundance of bathing: I have been taken to the Casino to see the fashionable life of a French resort from midnight to four of the day, and from the Casino to a frightfully expensive Russian cabaret where I drank champagne and watched fantastical dances and heard quaint old Russian songs till six o'clock: I have had a fortnight of good tennis, on the same courts as Mlle. Suzanne Lenglen and Count Salm (of Vienna) and Borotra—who all but won the men's championship of the world the other day in U.S.A.—and a host of other

notabilities are wont to use: I have crossed the Spanish
border, and seen a bullfight: I have been taken down to the
costly tea rooms for "porto-flips," and afternoon teas, and
cocktails: I have gone to the dear little old town of Bayonne
and explored a cathedral of the xiii century, the most part of
which was built by our own Black Prince.

I have gone for a long walk southward on the coast
toward the border of Spain with Jim—and two stray Great
Danes whom Jim's love for all dogs insisted should be allowed
to accompany us—to a little village called Bidart not far from
another little coast-village, St Jean-de-Luz, where the greatest
monarch of France, and I think of modern times, the golden
Louis Quatorze (XIV), took in marriage the Infanta Maria
Therésa of Spain, and after the ceremony commanded that the
entrance of that church should be forever walled up: "for
none," said he, "shall ever hereafter pass by this portal and by
any subsequent unhappiness in their wedded life, cast the
shadow of gloom upon the path which our royal felicity has
made a path of honor and joy." I have, besides seen an Opera
Comique as the guest of the rich maiden aunt who makes the
fifth of our family party, and whom I have twice accompanied
on after-dinner promenades in the stormy evenings of this
Biscayan coast, and heard with patience to the end of her long
tale of Boston maiden-auntly distresses.

What more I have done is of too trifling a nature to set
down, item by item, for my pen, which is ready enough in
describing a bull fight or a tennis tournament, lacks subtlety
to convey the general effect of happiness, animation, beauty,
vigor, rest, work and play, which a thousand nameless,
unremembered deeds and duties through the day, all combine
to give my holiday.

Do not think that because I have tasted fashionable life
and cocktails, I hereafter shall model my life on the one and
nourish it on the other! I had some thought within myself
before my birthday of making you the promise totally to
abstain from wines & spirits: I was perfectly open to decide
one way or the other according as the reasons pro or con

appeared the stronger. And I decided that, as I was (probably) to move in a society where wine is used and not abused, it might often appear churlish in me to say "I am a total abstainer," so that I would do myself no good in others' eyes.

To load myself with such rigid rules appeared, moreover, to be unnecessary, as I think that I shall not be greatly tempted in this respect; so that it appeared to profit me but little. And as for the ethics of the thing, per se and propter se, I see no argument whatever for abstinence. The only reason that I could see to have any weight was that you and Mother might be easier if your wild and feckless son had imposed upon himself this one restraint.

But on further reflection it came into my mind that you both had sufficient confidence in his general uprightness and decency to let him "gang his ain gait" in details, you having done your very good best for the solidity of his character by and large. So that's that. Because, you see (as the joint consuls of Rome always so divided their authority that when their votes differed, "his who said NO was held to carry more weight than his who said YES") the arguments were all against such action.

These were not the only serious reflections that occupied me at that same time. What am I to be? and what shall I do in life? You know I am great on "periods of life," and set great store on beginnings of things, like birthdays, and terms, and New Year's Day, and months and seasons. One of the verses that once I saw in Mother's "bathroom calendar" at home,—

Every day is a fresh beginning,
Listen, my soul to the glad refrain,
And, spite of old sorrows and frequent sinning,
And errors repeated, and subsequent pain,
Take heart with the day and begin again —

has appealed to me more than almost any other, because I itch always to do one thing at a time, to begin, continue, and end it as a unit, and able, in retrospect, to say "One thing I

did, and I did it whole." But I could get no better reply to the
question "What shall I be?" than the somewhat indefinite one,
that I hoped to be a great headmaster: that I would shape my
next years toward that end, and embrace all possible
opportunities for testing my ability in that capacity: and that,
failing that, I would take to some other profession as the Bar
or the University. I have a great respect for the "professional
class:" there is ample room for them in Canada, where
Jingoism at present finds an extraordinarily fruitful field,
fertilized by the ignorance of the population; and simply to be
"an educated man," with comfortable enough an income to
withstand the bullying of popular prejudice, would seem to me
a fair ambition in life.

A letter from Cyril Bailey yesterday gave me the news
that, provisionally, I shall have to share a sitting room with
Louis Alexander MacKay, M.A. Rhodes Scholar from Ontario.
I'm not overjoyed: MacKay is eccentric, frightfully clever, an
artist and poet, and three or four years my senior. Also, he
does not (as yet) play many games, although he is extremely
well built, tall and handsome. In Balliol he may shine with
uncommon lustre, as he has always done in Toronto. On the
other hand, his career of brilliance may have played itself out.
From what I saw of him at Trinity, I find it difficult to
forecast the nature of our alliance. I hope all will be well; at
all events, the experiment has the interest of mystery to
recommend it to me!...

Jim is now in bed. I have been reading so much of
Stevenson lately that I'm afraid this reads like *The Master of
Ballintrae* or *Catriona*! I shall be in my rooms at Balliol in 3
or 4 days, & shall then have leisure to write with more
deliberation to you.

Dearest love from Bill

[During this period Dorothy had been rather unwillingly placed
for two years in an English boarding school in Brighton – SMW]

"AT LAST I AM AT OXFORD"
(October—December, 1925)

SMW

Bill's life at Oxford was off to a good start. "After the chills of Trinity College," he wrote in his autobiography, "Balliol seemed bathed in effervescence, warmth and friendship. I entered it with joy, was soon invited to join the Boat Club and was made stroke of a Freshman Four which won a cup for each member and required me to make a short speech to a crowded hall at the St. Catherine's Day dinner." He made friends easily, including Mason Hammond, who was later best man at our wedding, Donald McDougall, a Canadian who had been blinded in the first world war, and Crown Prince Olaf of Norway, who rowed in the same "Eight" as Bill.

Meanwhile, realizing that Bill was assured of three years in England, his mother took Dorothy and Moll to England in 1925 to renew old family ties and put Dorothy, then seventeen, in a girl's school at Brighton for two years. His mother and Moll then returned to Winnipeg in time for Christmas. Ironically, Moll, who was to finish her college work in Canada, wished to stay in England or France, while Dorothy longed to return to her teenage life in Winnipeg. Moll managed to break her ankle on Christmas day, and suffered considerably from it and from the disruption of her plans.

Bill, on the other hand, was able to arrange a delightful three week Christmas holiday with Dorothy when they visited relatives, and also stayed for a week in "unusual comfort and formality" with Lady Drury, widow of a distinguished British admiral, and her sister. While Bill was by this time "woefully behind in every aspect" of his studies and worked during much of his vacation, he also found time for "the novelty of the billiard table and tea dances at neighboring houses."

LETTERS

> Balliol College, Oxford
> Sunday Morning, 4.x.1925

My Dear Pater

At length and at last, I am at Oxford.

I could find it in me to shift to another time some description of the quiet beauty of it all; but the wide gravel walk between two dewy lawns is now half-covered with ruddy brown leaves that fell overnight from the two massive chestnuts that stand sentinel by my study window. At every gentle gust, these two great beings rustle as though whispering their hurried good-bye to the hundred withering leaves that straightway break their stems and flutter, flutter, flutter to the ground.

Yesterday the left-hand tree was richly clad in its broad leaves of green and golden yellow; this morning half its foliage reposes on the ground. Through its black branches I get a fair good view of Trinity, which tomorrow will be plainer yet. The children that passed beneath them yesterday, or played in the dead leaves while their nurses sat down in the seat which kings and governors, prelates and barons, have flung themselves upon, or used to read on in the summer terms—these children stop to gather the shining brown chestnuts.

And not they alone, for five minutes past I saw Cyril Bailey and the Master (I think), A.D. Lindsay, clad in pyjamas, slippers and bathrobe, with a towel flung over the shoulder, stride rustling across the leaf-strewn path on their way back from the showers. They, too, stopped to gather chestnuts, and I heard Cyril's infectious laugh as he found an extra good one...

After breakfast I am going for a long walk to see the lie of Oxford and to visit some quaint old churches. Do you know

Iffley? or Cowley? or Sandford, Nuneham, Baldon, Dorchester, Wallingford, Bensington, or Ewelme? These are all on a route which my book on "Near Oxford" describes, and I shall follow as far as I feel inclined today.

At 4^{30} Kenneth Bell, a history don who is very keen on rowing and extremely humorous and funny, has invited me to tea at his house. McDougall, the blind man from Toronto, who got a special grant from the Rhodes Trust, is "up" (i.e. in college). None of the other men are known to me so far.

Goodbye, dear Father: often you will think of me. For my part, you are always in my thoughts at times like this, when there is such a feast of beauty that one alone cannot enjoy it, and when also the future holds something of dread that one alone feels at times a little daunted. Still, I am keen to do well: my tutors are keen to help me, and perhaps keenness and labour will compensate for brilliance!

Your affect. son, Wilfred W.

Balliol College, Oxford
Sunday night, 11.x.1925

[To his mother]

This will let you know that on Friday the 2nd I entered my rooms on Staircase XV of Balliol. Last Sunday I started immediately after breakfast to visit Iffley Church, a mile away: the old place was so fascinating—it was built in pure Norman style, in the days of Thomas à Becket—that I stayed there till long past lunch time.

On Thursday my study-mate, L.A. MacKay, the Ontario Rhodes, arrived. His brilliance will very appreciably assist me, I trust. Heaven knows, I need much and able assistance! My tutors are A.W. Pickard-Cambridge, an authority of note on Demosthenes, & Cyril Bailey. For the latter I have to write a 6-page essay on no less a subject than the origin of the Homeric Poems. This subject was dished out to me in the most offhand manner, although it necessitates the reading of voluminous volumes. Except that the burden of work is dreadfully depressing to contemplate, I find Oxford in all things more delightful than words have power to describe. From the early morning, when the "Scout" (= valet. In Cambridge they are "gyps") with elaborate noisiness comes in to take my boots, pour out hot water for shaving, pull the blind up, and then say "It's five an' twenty to h'eight, sir"—to the clear cold chimes of midnight, when I toss my book aside on the sofa & gather myself for a final "warm" before the dying fire: then, in a burst of determination, dash up to my "coffin" & bed—the day is a great cycle of labour & jollity & peaceful autumnal beauty...

Love from Bill

Balliol College, Oxford
Friday 13.xi.1925

My dear Pater

It is eleven o'clock at night, and a frosty, misty night at that, in mid November. In the Common Room are four men reading the papers before a dying fire. Through the open windows comes the sound of revelry across the quad from Hall, and the shouts of merrymakers pursuing one another about the paths mingles with the music of the band in Hall. And why all the excitement? you ask. Tonight, then, if you must know, is the night of the "Morrison Dinner."

The "Morrison Fours" are the races rowed by freshmen in "clinker four" boats with fixed seats. I was appointed stroke of one of these a month ago, and our crew yesterday raced the first heat. Winning that, we entered the finals, and as my crew again won, it fell to me to reply to the toast of the evening, "To the winning Morrison Four." I did the whole business fairly well, I believe: at least, escaping unnoticed in the crowd that pressed out of Hall, I overheard several remarks that made me feel extraordinarily pleased with myself: and fellows have dropped in one by one, or in knots of two or three, to congratulate me.

I write to tell you this in case, when Sunday comes, my memory is dulled, or my time is short. I think you will rejoice in my success—both athletic in winning the Fours, and polite,

in making the reply: the assembly of old oarsmen from
Balliol—earls or barons & baronets ad lib—for this is the
centenary of Balliol rowing, 1825-1925—was formidable, but
now that all has gone off so well I retire gladly to bed. At 7^{30} I
have a cavalry parade!

Your affectionate son,
Wilfred Westgate

Baliol College
Oxford
15.xi.25

My dear Pater:

Friday's excited letter must suffice to tell you the chief
news of the week...I am afraid that Mother's visit here pulled
me back not a little in my work: a week has passed since she
left, however, & as I worked very hard in the course of it I am
now almost abreast of essays and lectures. I have a weekly
essay—not to say weakly!—on general subjects—Dr. Johnson,
Gothic Architecture, Education in England, Nationalism,
George Eliot, and the like—which I read on Saturdays before
3 other men & a don. Hereafter—for this term, the don is to
be no less than A. D. Lindsay himself, the Master. I have also
an essay on Classical subjects, which I read before Cyril
Bailey with MacKay & a man, Murrie. For this week we were
asked to select our own subjects; & Murrie & I having both by
chance selected Greek vases, MacKay, to keep the series on
the subject of vases & flasks, is writing an essay on their
contents!

Mother sails on Friday. I shall probably go up to London
to see her onto the boat train, but the arrangements of an
examiner & other considerations may prevent me. I know that
she has seats reserved, & all arrangements well in hand, so
that I shall be the less anxious about her & Moll.

Dearest love from
Bill

Balliol
20.xi.1925

My dearest Mother:

With infinite patience I have gone into the deep problems of finance that seem always to dog my path, and the results of my patience are set forth on another page—or rather alas! the wasted paper on six other pages. This note is simply to say goodbye to you.

A year ago tomorrow (when you sail), you sent me word of my election to the Rhodes. And here the circling year has left us where a year ago it promised: I in Oxford, and you five thousand miles away. I never hoped indeed that you would be able to come and help me settle in, or that Moll could pass a fortnight with me. It has been very nice for us all: and now I think it is very nice that you should be going back to Pater.

In athletics I have got well started (I wish that you could see my silver cup[1] for stroking the Morrison Four! In studies I am dreadfully backward, but I am in the most favourable circumstances for making progress; and in other respects I have good friends and great associations, so that I should do well in everything. I shall indeed try to, and I know that you and Pater at home will help me, and be glad when I do well and sorry when I fall—I shall try to do well.

Your loving son
Wilfred Westgate

[1] It was a pewter mug—SMW.

Balliol College, Oxford
Sunday 6.xii.1925

My dear Pater:

You will be glad to hear that term is over, and that now I am free to work as, and when, and where, I will, without the officious attentions of tutors and lectures and regular hours! I had a "collection," or terminal test, in Cicero's Orations yesterday, and tomorrow morning go to Cyril Bailey to see the result of it. The questions were from speeches which I have never read, so that I did them all at sight. I think, however, that I got them right. After seeing Cyril, I go in cap & gown to Hall, where the Master sits in state, and perform what is called "Handshaking." My tutor, Pickard-Cambridge, leads me up to the dais, introduces me to the Master, comments (I fear only too unfavourably) on my term's work, and then, after I have shaken hands with the Master, lets me go.

The task of appraising your work is taken very seriously by tutors; and, as they neither fear God nor regard man, but say exactly what they think, they can make it very unpleasant for the slothful. I shall tell you next Sunday what "Picker" has to say about me!

A most charming old miracle play was acted in Hall last week—The Towneley Annunciation, The Towneley Second Shepherd's Play,[1] and an anonymous play of the Adoration of the Magi & of the wrath of Herod, were all combined to make one mediæval Nativity play. A more touching and yet quaint and funny picture of Christmas festivity in England in 1200 or so I could not conceive.

A concealed organ plays a quaint old ditty, while the Hall is in perfect darkness, except where the flickering light of two open hearths breaks the total blackness. Suddenly a light appears high up near the roof, behind curtains. The curtains are drawn back, and a gigantic figure in white, flowing beard with a gilt halo about his head, and regal robes of scarlet & ermine, announces in rhyming lines that he is God: he is at war with Hell & Satan: he has suffered Adam to be tortured in Hell for nigh five thousand years: now he sends his Son to work his deliverance; to which end he commands his servant Gabriel to take his sacred message to Mary. <u>Curtain.</u>

At the moment the heavens are closed, we see, down on Earth, the starry messenger Gabriel speaking to Mary; and shortly afterward the doubts and distress of Joseph, who walks to and fro upon the stage, soliloquizing in great trouble. But a light shines down from Heaven, and Gabriel is seen again telling Joseph the truth. <u>Curtain.</u>

An aged shepherd, bent & crippled, hobbles on to the stage bewailing the cold & his rheumatism, and the poor markets: a middle-aged one follows soon afterwards, and they sing a song in desperately bad voices! until a third & young shepherd comes on the scene. In order (I suppose) that the spectators may be <u>quite</u> sure that these are shepherds, a farcical & quite irrelevant scene is put in about a sheep-stealer who steals a sheep while they are sleeping on the ground, & taking the sheep home, bids his wife conceal it in the cradle!

In the morning, the peasants come round & search the house; but as the poor wife groans & rolls on the floor, & bids them not harm her newborn babe in the cradle, they pass on without finding the lost sheep. But suddenly the old shepherd cries out, "Hast thee given nae pence to the newly born bairn?" No, they have quite forgotten to do that! so back they run, & the youngest insists on putting his penny into the baby's hand! The scene is uproarious: Father gesticulates & stammers & protests,—"He weeps an he wakes!" and Mother cries she had rather <u>eat</u> the darling in the crib than have him disturbed! But the fraud is discovered, & the struggling wether is hauled out, & the robber is sewn in a sack & drowned! <u>Curtain.</u>

The shepherds (we are supposed to be assured that they are bona-fide shepherds by this time!), settle down to sleep, see a vision of angels which sing in the gallery, and on waking start off "to Bedlam-town in Galilee!" Three perambulations round the stage are taken to represent the road "to Bedlam-town of Galilee," and they knock at the door which, hitherto, has done duty for the sheep stealer's door, but which now opens to show the stable and the child. There is a most touching tableau here, when the young shepherd offers the baby a ball, & bids him "go to the tennis." <u>Curtain.</u>

A prodigious, hectoring individual in golden robes & a golden panama hat (supposed to be a crown!) swaggers on to the stage, followed by two knights in feudal armour, & roars out "I am the greatest king in Jewry land, and I am Herod the king!" An unrehearsed effect was produced by the lance of one of the knights accidentally catching in the brim of the panama hat, & giving it a rakish tilt; but Herod recovered his presence of mind, & after a lot more braggart bellowing, subsided on a bench at one side of the stage & kept still.

Meanwhile three kings (led by a star which an angel, who now appears in Heaven high above, holds above the versatile doorway) walk up the aisle through the middle of the audience, & mounting the stage, begin to soliloquize aloud, till Herod's butler overhears them, & brings them to the king. They are dispatched to find the child, do so, & worship him, & being warned by another angel, depart another way.

Herod is apprised of their deceit, & sends his 2 knights to spear the children, which they do with great gusto, & to the deep distress of two Rachels (dressed one in pea green, the other in red, like medieval nuns), but to the amusement of the audience. Herod is very pleased, orders a feast, & calls to his minstrels for a merry tune. What do you think is played by way of a "merry tune" for the amusement of Herod the King? "Good Christian men, rejoice!"

But the tune has hardly begun when a skeleton, "God's messenger, Death," leaps into the stage & kills the wicked king. The aforesaid versatile door opens, disclosing this time a burning fiery furnace (made of flame-coloured paper): and out of the furnace crawls the Devil himself!

With hellish outcries & gestures, he seizes the dead bodies & flings them into the furnace, while the door closes again and, alone with Death, we ponder the mystery of the Nativity, till the lights all die, the quaint air, played by the invisible organ at the beginning, is played again, and so the mumming is all over.

How you would have loved it! or your Indian children, or Africans! Someday I shall return to Canada, and go to Port Hope or Upper Canada [schools] & introduce these things: for lovely & fascinating as they are to the ear & eye, they have a double spiritual value, in that they take us back to the solemn night in the original "Bedlam town"—not in Galilee, though! —and also in that they give us a spiritual communion with the pious and devout and naive, but very jolly generations of our own people who lived in our own country before Canada was known.

I am staying in college till Dec 23rd, when I go to Lady Drury, Tenterden, Kent for 10 days. (Dorothy, I hope, will come on the 28th for a week). We may then go to Salisbury,— to which I was invited, but too late for Christmas Day,— or Kingsclere. Tomorrow, however, I go to London for 2 days holiday as the guest of Miss Sands, the funny American old maid who stayed with us at Biarritz this summer. What a portentous letter!

from your affectionate son Bill.

[1] Towneley Plays: 32 miracle plays preserved in late 15th century manuscript by the Towneley family of Lancashire and intended for production by the crafts of Wakefield.

Balliol College, Oxford
13.xii.1925

My dear Pater

I know this will not reach you in time for Christmas: but I do not think that you will need any letter of mine to wish you all a happy Christmas. But, though I do not _need_ any letter of yours to wish me the same, I should very much _like_ one; and so I will write this one, late as it is.

"Handshaking." As anyone who knows Oxford will at once conclude, the one thing that is not done at "handshaking" is the shaking of hands! but on the same principle as the May races fall in June, and as "Collections" is the name given to examinations where nothing is collected, handshaking is called by its name. My handshaking, I am most happy to say, passed off extremely well. I was called up to the dais, and sat at one side of a long table opposite the master, who had Pickard-Cambridge on one hand and Cyril on the other.

Picker, being my tutor, began. "I find Mr. Westgate, Master, a much better Latin than a Greek scholar. The Latin Proses I have given him have been done in a very good style, and he has some taste in the matter of Latin literature. But the Greek show a certain immaturity, and ignorance of ordinary grammatical forms, such as is commonly found only in the schools in this country. There appears also a certain hastiness about much of his work, as though it were done often at the last minute, and in a great hurry. Mr Bell (the lecturer at Queen's College in Demosthenes) tells me that he only did one paper out of three this term—though in that one he got α [alpha]."

Here the master enquired why I had missed two papers. "One, sir," I explained, "was when my mother was here." "Oh, yes, I see," he replied, but Picker put in a characteristic remark "Ah, yes, of course: parents are a thing to be sternly discouraged!" Cyril then said something nice about my essays, which I thought had been ghastly failures, but which evidently pleased him. The master then said that he was glad I was doing well, that I must look to my elementary Greek work, and no doubt I should soon fit into the scheme of things very well. Picker again put in a pleasant word, "Of course, Master, Mr. Westgate has been playing his part in the College life"—referring to my rowing and running, I suppose—and then I was dismissed.

I have given you as nearly accurate a report as I can of my handshaking, not because it was remarkably brilliant, but so that you can see both what my tutors think of me, and also how thoroughly they do take stock of every move one makes in the term, how closely they analyze your mistakes and prescribe for your needs, and how quite outspoken they are of their thoughts. I, being near the end of the alphabet, was the last one called up, and could hear something of the reports that the other men got. Some had most enviable reports,— MacKay among others: but some again visibly squirmed in their chair, and one could catch words like "careless," and "lack of interest," and "insufficient energy,"—though these words were always in a much lower tone, I thought—and the poor wretches walked out of the Hall like Haman from the king's palace. In my Cicero "collection" I got β⁺, which was the

same as MacKay and—considering that I did all at sight—I
felt very pleased...

I am reading hard in Latin and Greek and French. Often
the longing comes upon me to heave Demosthenes, Cicero,
Virgil and Livy into my grate and kindle the pile. Why should
man spend these pleasant years in elucidating the obscure
and uninteresting and stilted verbiage of the Aeneid, when
after all his labour he has grasped mere rubbish? It may be
good training,—but am I to spend life training for a conflict
for which I shall be too old to enter? Am I to be nothing
better, at the age of 50, than a poor old dithering grinder with
whom I read Virgil in town these days? waxing angry at a free
and vivid rendering of Virgil, which he says must be turned
into flowing and pompous English, talking deeply about "the
smooth felicity of Ovid," while he shivers before a dying fire,
and hasn't the sense to put on more coal! And he, thirty years
ago, was a scholar of Balliol, and won—pah! the Gaisford
prize for Latin verse! I'd rather be a dog and bay the moon
than such a howling ninny!

As I say, however, I am reading French, and have even, in
a dilettante fashion, done a little Spanish. There are some
lovely sea ballads and sonnets in a book of Spanish verse
which a Scottish friend of mine showed me the other day. In
the comparative leisure of Lady Drury's I shall try to write
something for the *Free Press*: anything to keep alive! to realize
that Virgil, in the world of today, counts for rather less than a
knowledge of plumbing, and that Cicero was but a petti-
fogging lawyer with the vulgar vainglory of a middleclass
politician.

You will be glad to hear that I got through "Divvers"—the
Divinity exam in the Greek of Matthew & John, and the
English of Acts. The reason that I have to take this is that I
have decided to take "Mods."[1] in March, 1927, not 1926. It
may necessitate a fourth year at Oxford, or it may mean going
down without a degree: but at least it will mean a thorough
and leisurely (in the sense that I shall have opportunity to
read widely, & beyond mere texts) digestion of all that I do read.

The Classics B.A. is given after two exams, "Honour Moderations," usually at the end of 2 years, and "Final Schools," (or "Greats") at the end of 4 years. MacKay is taking "Mods" in 1 year, a thing which I hoped to do originally, but which I have now decided against: so that unless I take "Schools" in one year after "Mods," I must either go down without a degree, or spend a fourth year here. But things will right themselves hereafter...

With dearest love to you all,

Bill

[1] The colleges which make up Oxford University vary in size. Balliol, the second oldest, was founded in 1263. Normally it has around 80 students. The Oxford educational system differs considerably from those in the United States and Canada, and from most other English universities. Instead of attending classes in which students listen to a lecturer, the Oxford student prepares long papers himself and reads them before his tutor and two or three other students, followed by discussion and advice. A student must prepare for several examinations each year by reading widely in many subjects under the guidance of a tutor. There are also University lectures given by well-known professors and visiting scholars. Students are responsible for attending those most important to their field.

"Mods" is defined by the *Oxford English Dictionary* as colloquial for "Moderations," the name of the First Public Examination for the degree of B.A. conducted by the Moderators. "Mods" is taken at the end of the first or second year at college, depending on the student's readiness. The examination called "Greats" (officially "Literæ Humaniores") is the final examination at the end of the third or fourth year. It consists of eleven papers of several hours each writen over the course of several days. These are scored by two examiners, each independently grading with the Greek letters alpha, beta, gamma or delta. Greats is then concluded by a "Viva," or oral examination. The student receives an Honours class of first, second, third or fourth, according to the number of alphas, betas, etc. received.

— XI —
"A VERY PLEASANT PUPIL"
(January—July, 1926)

Balliol College, Oxford
Sunday: 16.i.1926

My dear Moll:

Back to the old J.C.R. [Junior Common Room] again,— and on the whole very glad to get back. Not that I did not love Lady Drury and her quaint old sister, and the golf and billiards and dances at Tenterden; not that I got tired of Salisbury, where I played golf with Kathleen, and had teas with the Luckhams, and went to a *thé dansant* in the New Forest, and had long talks with Hubert, whom I really think is a prince of a fellow, from the time when Uncle John & Aunt Beatrice were packed off from Audley House, about 10 o'clock, until midnight or one; not that I did not enjoy the laborious reading that I did both at Salisbury and Tenterden. But one finds it very jolly to get back to one's rooms...

I had two "colleccers" (collections, i.e.: terminal exams) on Friday, on Demosthenes & Sophocles. Demosthenes went quite well: the other was painfully hard. But this term I feel much better equipped, in the way of experience, for the problem of planning my work. I get up at 7^{30} and go to chapel at 8^{05} and then to breakfast at 8^{15}. Immediately after that I go to the Union, where there is one warm room—in Balliol there is not even one—& stay until lunch time. After lunch I shall row, when rowing starts, until tea time, & then return to the Union till 7^{30}. After dinner I shall probably read in my room, or the Camera [reading room of Bodleian Library], when I am not too busy with bridge or talking or taking coffee.

Oxford this weekend presents a remarkable appearance. When I was coming up on Thursday, a little snow was falling. On Friday morning the ground was white, covered with two or three inches of snow. The storm lasted all Friday, stopped and resumed again, and now, on Sunday morning, has covered the ground with over 9 inches of snow! The scenery is lovely: the perfect silence of the quads is made more silent still: the bare trees have loads of snow on every bough: the roofs are blanketed, and bells sound clear & sharp through the cold air. We want to get a bob sleigh or toboggan, but the whole of Oxford seems not to contain one of either. I am writing to Dave to send me skates; he can get them cheaply about the end of February, & send them to me for use next winter: then I shall try to go to Switzerland with the hockey team.

With much love from Bill

Oxford College Union
Sunday: 31.1.1926

My dear Mother

I am not seriously perplexed about my work here. I shall stick strenuously to classics, at least until I have written Hon. Mods. next March. By that time I shall have read the bulk of all the chief ancient authors, & I hope also not a little of the writers of all periods in French & English literature. I shall therefore have a wide panorama before me, & shall see what part of it all appeals to me most. Besides the appeal of pleasure or interest, I must consider the practical utility of the various branches of study, & combining both considerations, I shall be likely to choose wisely. Perhaps, too, I shall be able to come home in the summer following Mods (1927) & talk the thing over both with the dons in Toronto & Winnipeg, & with you & Father.

With love from Bill

SMW

The following undated letter, written shortly before Bill's April, 1926 vacation, is reproduced in facsimile to show his handwriting and artistic sense of humor.

JUNIOR COMMON ROOM.

Walter has been here for Thursday. Fri. Sat. Sun., and will go home tomorrow.

BALLIOL COLLEGE,
OXFORD.

Sunday .

Dear Moll :

Just a note to say

that I hope you are getting on

allright with your 'globigerinae'

and marine raspberries. I have

one week of desperate and

frantic labour ahead of me,

before I regain a few weeks'
of liberty -

In the riding School, we
have had several days of
jumping, & I, after a dozen
hurdles, feel quite at home.
If only you lean
well forward
at one moment,

and well back
the next, and the
sergeant

does not crack
his whip at the

wrong time, you land quite

safely. Most people struck

quite unconventional attitudes

when they

ended the leap,

some poised themselves
in an inverted position
on the horses head for

a giddy second, before they
fell, with a
sounding thump, to
the ground. Some fell off before
they got near the hurdle; others
backed into it, kicked it down, &
triumphantly trampled it! So far
I have myself enjoyed the fun. Good
luck in the Exams ———— Bill.

at Sandcroft, Redhill
21.iii.26

My dear Mother

A good deal has happened this week; to get it all straight I'll begin at Sunday and come down chronologically. But as there is nothing noteworthy to chalk against Sunday, I must describe our party on Monday.

I had a dancing lesson on Monday afternoon, and at 4^{30} went down to London with McDougall, the blind man, and put up at a pleasant enough little dump called the "Manor Hotel" near Paddington. We were due for dinner at the Earl & Countess of Clarendon's place at 8^{30}, so at 7 we began to take hot baths and shave and dress. My confrère's first discovery was that he had left his dinner waistcoat at Oxford, and must now choose between wearing a brown tweed one or none at all. As I was wearing "tails," however, & therefore a white waist-coat, I lent him my dinner waistcoat, & we sailed off merrily enough at 8^{15}, directing our taxi driver to Pitt House, Hampstead.

The house is dreadfully difficult to find, and our chariot did not get to the door till a little after the dinner hour—a painful position enough to me, but inevitable considering the difficulty of piloting the blind man. The dinner was quite an informal affair, and began as soon as we arrived and were introduced to our host & hostess.

Bonnycastle and a South African were the only other men guests, but there was a Russian girl, a Princess of some description, and four other girls. One was exceedingly nice, the others I hardly saw; for at the end of dinner they all retired to prepare for the ball, while we sat over our port, and yarned with the Earl of sailing cruises in the Mediterranean. About half-past ten, we drove off to St. James' Square in two motors, the ladies in one and we in a second,—an open Austin, I think, which his lordship drove in person, I sitting up beside him. He is a very entertaining person, some 6 feet 6 in height, and broad in proportion, but made to limp rather

clumsily by one leg being—by accident, I suppose, or wound-
ing—inches shorter than the other.

We drove up to Lady Astor's house and piled out, then
went up a canvas-covered stairway to the hall where our coats
were to be checked. Half a dozen lackeys in plum coloured
uniforms strapped across and across with gold brocade, and
caught at the knee with bunches of ribbon, relieved us of our
garments, and we passed into a further hall where a broad
stairway led upwards to the ballroom. McD. and I went up
with a good many others streaming in the same direction, and
at the top met Lady Clarendon & one or two of the girls of our
party: the rest were not in sight, so we passed along the
passageway to the ballroom, where Lady Astor, brilliant with
a most glorious tiara of diamonds & pearls, met us. She is
incredibly lively & jolly, and fairly skipped about, making
jokes and pulling people about and turning this way & that to
talk to everybody at once.

I had McD. by the arm, & was just waiting for Lady Astor
to turn toward us so that Lady Clarendon could introduce us
both, when I spotted a rather short, fair-haired person half
facing us, and chatting, I think, to Bonnycastle. "Is it, really?"
I said to myself: "so it is." At that moment Lady Astor
extricated herself from a knot of people & came up to us.

"Lady Clarendon, so glad you've got here, and brought at
least a remnant of your party. Where have you lost the rest?
This is Mr. McDougall? how do you do? in five minutes you
will be crushed to death, Mr. McDougall, but I'm so glad of
meeting you before your lamented end! and Mr. Westgate,
how do you do? what have you done with your partners?"

Immediately she bobbed away and tugged the fair-haired
person by the arm, nearly upsetting him. "Sir, will you come
this way? may I introduce you—Mr. Westgate—The Prince of
Wales,— Mr. McDougall." And in a flash she was away again.
"How do you do?" said H.R.H. Where do you come from? "I
come from Winnipeg, sir." "Oh, Winnipeg, yes, Winnipeg!
Remember that very well. Should like to go out there again
some time." He exchanged a few more sentences and then

Lady Astor whirled up again and dragged him off & left McD. & me to find our partners & dance...

About 2³⁰ Lady Clarendon began to collect her party. We rather dragged ourselves away—though really the end of the dance was in sight—and said goodbye to everybody rather reluctantly. Lady Clarendon hoped that we should see her again, if we were ever near Pitt House. Who knows? perhaps we shall...

Love from Bill

SMW

Bill left Oxford to spend his spring vacation in France with the McKaigs. Illness caused him to return late to Balliol.

Balliol College
Sunday, 2.v.26

Dearest Father

...On Sunday [April 25th] I left Tours & that afternoon crossed the Channel. And here is a wonder; and wonder of wonders: though such storms lashed the Channel as have hardly been known since the White Ship (the old boat that somebody never smiled again about), I was not sea-sick! Hooray!

Monday (the first day of term) I spent with Aunt Kathleen, and in shopping in London, at the Army & Navy— In virtue of my scholarship, I may say, I am an honorary member of the Army & Navy Stores. Then I came up to Oxford, and found MacKay with a crackling fire and a stack of *Globes* (*Toronto Daily Globe*) two feet high.

On Tues. I saw Picker, and the doctor. The former gave me examinations to take, the latter pills: he also said that my stomach had lost its tone—what <u>does</u> he mean by the tone of a stomach? He thumped it diligently and listened to the various bass notes it echoed, and then delivered himself of this remark. I suppose he expected it to vibrate like the body of a violincello, and was disappointed at its being sharper or flatter than it ought—He also said that it had been strained

(—no, <u>not</u> by eating) and advised me not to row this term. I have not been asked to row, so that this entails no privation.

It was natural for me to think that as I had come back late, and so missed collections (terminal exams) on Fri. and Saturday, I should be excused them altogether—I reckoned without my host. In a nice hypocritical voice I said to Picker on Tuesday morning, "It's rather sad that I should miss collections like this—" "Oh but you won't miss them," he burst in, "I've got a Demosthenes paper ready for you, and on Thursday you can take a Greek plays paper!" I did them both, and got "β⁺", (that is, "beta plus") on the one and "β⁺" on the other, which Picker subsequently changed to "α" (alpha). Alpha is an almost impossible mark with Picker, and β⁺ is very good indeed, so that I feel thoroughly happy about everything in general, and my work in particular...

Love from Bill

Balliol College, Oxford
Sunday, 16.v.1926

My dearest Father,

I got a great shock when I saw your telegram on my table last Sunday, but Moll's letter will have explained everything: I shall try to give you direct word of myself every week hereafter. At the sight of the brown telegraph-envelope I thought that Lady Drury must be threatened with lynching, for the previous Monday I wired her "If I can be of any help, please telegraph. Otherwise, I spectate."[1] Immediately my thoughts turned to battle, and I pictured myself hewing a path through ranks of angry strikers, and felling their threatening Wat Tyler[2] with one blow of my fist, and releasing her ladyship from the creaking rope that attached her neck to the high oak limb. Pressure was brought to bear on the Prime Minister, and in the Court Circular of 1927, January 1ˢᵗ, Mr. R.I.W. Westgate had the honour to be promoted above astrologers, magicians, Chaldeans and counsellors and made Satrap of the Province of Manitoba and cup bearer to Nebuchadnezzar the King. By your words my hopes were roughly dashed...

You still ask about writing to Pickard-Cambridge. I should think it would be a good thing to get the written opinion of a man of his judgment & experience on what progress (if any) he thinks I am making, in work and sports and general growth: nothing could be more natural than such an enquiry from a home five thousand miles away, & Picker would be very glad to have the opportunity of writing direct to you. Besides, it gives me a sort of extra liaison with him, & shows him that I am not a waif pushed off to Oxford to struggle against examiners, but have a family who are interested enough in my doings to ask my tutor for his opinions of them...

Mason Hammond suggests that he might come with me [to France this summer]. I hope he will, for he is one of the best men I have ever met. The McKaigs, last summer, gave me my first introduction to New England Americans, & a very pleasant one it was. Of all the queer people in Oxford & Balliol, I like the New Englander best as a type. He is thoroughly open, and firm in his convictions: he is outspoken, which Eton and Harrow men are too polite to be: he is not temperamental, but can always be depended upon to stick to his convictions, however narrow they may be. He is not a rough diamond: he is not a Ciré pearl, but he is a very solid & genuine diamond, hard & inflexible but clear and sound all through. Canadians are often out for what they can get. Englishmen spend their lives turning up their noses—like Punch's cartoon of "Suburbia." South Africans approximate most to New Englanders...

Your affectionate son, Bill

[1] A general strike had been called in England.

[2] Wat Tyler: (d. 1381), English rebel and leader of the great peasant rebellion of 1381 in which mobs pillaged and burned public buildings and homes of government leaders.

To: Rev. T.B.R. Westgate

Balliol College,
Oxford
July 23/26

Dear Mr. Westgate,

Many thanks for your letter. Your son has always been a
very pleasant pupil to work with, and I was sorry that, owing
to our being short-handed last term, I had to send him to
someone outside (Mr. Bowra) for compositions, though Mr.
Bowra is an excellent scholar, & your son will not have lost by
the change.

When he came up, his work was full of inaccuracies of the
kind which one expects to be got over in the lower Forms of a
public school; to a great extent he has now got beyond these,
though they are always liable to recur, and probably any piece
of work which he does will have enough of them still to
prevent its being quite first class. But he has always worked
well, and has improved greatly all round in his work in the
year. I should think he ought to get a good 2nd class in Honour
Mods in March, though I should not like to discourage him
from making "a bid" for a First. On the other hand, if he has a
bad day, his work may easily drop to Third Class again. It is
difficult to prophesy, because he is not a very good examinee;
he is not very business-like in planning his time so as to cover
the ground, & is liable to get flurried. But he will have a good
Oral and practice in paper-work in his next two terms, & that
should help him to overcome this.

Whatever happens in the Examination, he will have
gained very much in learning sounder methods of work and
thought; and I should think he would gain even more by his
work for the Final School—Everyone here likes him and will
be glad to help him in any way.

Yours very truly

A. W. Pickard-Cambridge

— XII —
"I AM PHENOMENALLY LUCKY"
(July—October, 1926)

FROM A DIARY LETTER TO HIS FAMILY

Chetwynd Park, Newport
Salop. 21.vii.1926

Wed. 21st July

Was ever there seen so happy a person as I at this moment,
writing by the steady little flame of a white candle in a big
silver candlestick, under the shadow of a gigantic oaken
bedstead as big as my study in Winnipeg? Ten minutes ago
we were sitting in the drawing-room discussing the Shannon
and Trades Unions and Treason—handsome Mrs. Borough, a
most handsome Victorian lady of near seventy (who actually
was presented to the old Queen at court), her two daughters
(of whom the younger has been to Oxford, and both are most
awfully nice) and a most delightful Irish girl, Mrs. French,—
some connection with old Sir John.

Then ten struck: Miss Borough said she must go up to her
bath: Mrs. Borough planned how we should all visit the
bathroom tomorrow morning: the subject of bed was mooted,
discussed, & approved: the drawing-room was deserted,
candles were lit in the hall, & a procession made up the big
red-carpeted stairs. At the top, Mrs. Borough says she will
show me the bathroom, and candle in hand, I follow her to the
right, down a narrow passage.

"Just mind this step, Mr. Westgate, or you'll break your
leg and that will be sad: now here's a door,—I hope the
draught won't blow out your candle. No, that's right—well
done: now up a step and straight on. Oh no, not there,

straight on this way. Now turn to the left, about eight yards.
Yes. Then to the right—but, oh! mind that step down! and
through this door;—now can you squeeze past me? and
straight ahead down to the right. That door in front of you is
it."—and I find myself in a huge wooden-floored room, with a
great wood-encased bath built into one corner. I am comp-
limented on finding my way back again unaided, and again at
the head of the stairs, say goodnight to Mrs. Borough, and
walk in the opposite direction, turn left, and so reach my door.

How came I here? Miss MacDonald of the Isles introduced
me (by letter) to Mrs. Borough, & she sent me an invitation to
come here for July 21st to 31st. At 6^{30} this morning Aunt
Beatrice wakened me: at 7 Uncle John saw me out of the
house: at 11 I reached Oxford & saw several Canadian
students on tour, now lodging in Balliol (and, I may add, all
with reservations, of course,) making themselves thoroughly
obnoxious by their insolent, impertinent, and ungentlemanly
behaviour in college. At lunch with a Balliol man who has
been up all the vac., I heard descriptions of their shameless
conduct that made me blush for Canada, and particularly
Toronto. Then at 5^{26} I reached Newport, Salop. (= Shropshire).

A coachman & carriage were waiting for me at the country
station; the man touched his shiny hat: "You'm for Chetwynd
Park, Sir?" "Yes," I said: "good afternoon. Can you take my
trunk & bag with you, & my racquet?" "Yessir," and in a
minute we were off, rolling pleasantly through the village of
Newport, out on to the country road, till after a mile or two
we turned into a gateway. "Ga-a-a-ate," cried Jehu, and an old
woman came out to open the gate. On we rolled past dense
bushes of rhododendrons (no longer in bloom, of course), past
a hay field where two pheasants stopped & looked at us, past
a meadow where horses were grazing, past a gigantic
spreading old elm, & up to the house.

A cheerful sort of footman-factotem ushered me into the
hall, and then into the drawing room, where Mrs. Borough
was sewing. We had tea—then the three girls came in (two
daughters & Mrs. French). We walked in the gardens &

examined the roses & shrubs, the rockery, lawns, tennis court, and the pea-hen and her brood. At 7^{30} we change for dinner. At 8 we have dinner. At 9 in the drawing room we have coffee. We discuss presentations at court: I hold Mrs. Borough's wool for winding: we discuss the Shannon, Trades Unions, and Treason. At 10 we go to bed. At 11, this minute, I get undressed & get into bed.

Goodnight.

P.S. I write of this pleasant time because I think it will please you to hear of my pleasure; if you think it unfair that I should have such a disproportionate portion of happiness in comparison with you at home, consider first that I <u>am</u> phenomenally lucky. One Rhodes man in fifty does not have so good a time as I do. Consider, second, that my moments of happiness alternate with others of depression and anxious responsibility: consider third that my present happiness may (to some extent) be purchased at the price of future happiness, and that if I gad about now, carefree, in three year's time I may regret that I did not scorn these delights and live more laborious days. (I do not anticipate failure in exams, or that sort of thing: but I realize that I do not get so much work done in a summer spent like this as I should in a summer spent on a reading party.)

If I thought that my letters even tended to make you discontented, I should at once select as subjects for them the depressing and melancholy and distressing and unhappy periods of my weeks and terms; instead of selecting, as I try always to do, the pleasant & jolly ones when people are kind and the world seems very good.

Goodnight

Thursday: 22nd

The valet called me at 8 with hot water, gave me my letters, folded away my dinner clothes & set out my day ones. At 8^{30} the younger Miss Borough rapped on my door. "Bath ready," she cried, "I hope you can find your way!"

At 9 I went down to breakfast & found Mrs. Borough reading *The Morning Post*. I picked up the *Times,* selecting it from among the *Telegraph* and the *Times Literary Supplement*. Soon the rest of the party appeared, & breakfast went off with great jollity.

Retired about 9^{45} to the drawing-room to read & converse: at 10 I went to my room to write to Dorothy & Mrs. McKaig (who wants to cross with Dorothy & me next week), then read Cicero till 12^{30}. The three girls (2 Misses Borough & Mrs. French) & Mrs. Borough—she is the most handsome & young old lady I know—were weeding rose beds, so I helped for quarter of an hour, till a bell like a church bell rang for lunch.

We read and gossiped after lunch in the drawing-room, and at 3 went out to play tennis. The court looks beautiful, but is soft & mossy—lovely underfoot but slow to play upon. The girls are quite good. Tea at 5. Then a walk with two spaniels over the estate to examine the prize Wyandottes, & exercise the spaniels. Then the elder Miss Borough sang some French & German songs, and we had more tennis at 7.

When the loud bell again called us in (to dress, at 7^{30}) we found that Burton Borough, the son of dear old Mrs. Borough, & Mr. French, had returned from Chelmsford where they had been playing "the Cheshire Gentlemen" at cricket yesterday & today. Both men are 35 or so, and very nice, so we had a very jolly dinner and discussed countless things. The ladies retired about 8^{45} and we remained at our port for half an hour before rejoining them in the drawing-room. About ten they went to bed, while we stayed up till 11—the butler having brought us whisky & soda. The war stories that Borough (he is a capital story teller, very breezy, very rapid, very much to the point) tells of the Australians in Palestine, of his grandfather who ruled Chetwynd with an iron rod ("My old grandfather," says

Borough, "used to keep the servants on the *qui vive* very effectively. Every time he entered a fresh room,—if he came down from upstairs and went into the morning-room, he'd go straight up to the bell & ring it, then think of something to say when the man answered it"), of cricket, or Oxford, or farming,—all these were entrancing, & tired as I was, I felt sorry when French said something about bed.

Tomorrow I am to be shown "the King's chamber," where Charles the First slept for 3 days ("<u>nights</u> sounds less dissolute!) in the month of May, 1643—Also, there is to be a tennis party after lunch. Also, I am going to explore the grounds and read Cicero.

Goodnight

Friday: 23rd

An old Mrs Dobson drove over to tea with her two hawk-nosed maiden daughters to play tennis. The elder Miss Dobson & I had a long and stubborn set against the younger Miss Dobson & French, and lost.

Read Joseph Conrad all evening,—past 10 o'clock, when the family retired to bed, up to 11^{15} when I closed my book, turned down the lamp, lit my big white candle in its massive silver stand, bolted the drawing-room door, walked through the ante-room, bolted the ante-room, crossed the hall, ascended the stairs, blew out the hall lamp upstairs, & entered here.

Saturday: 24th

Burton Borough had to go to a County Council (Shropshire) meeting in <u>Shrewsbury</u> ("Shrews," by the way, rhymes with "toes" or "hose," not "pews") so I drove the 20 miles or so into Shrewsbury with him, was shown his club, & then left to myself for an hour and a half. The city is all but encircled by the Severn, which winds thus:

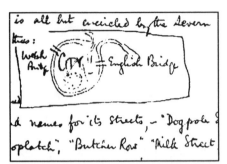

It has very quaint "black-and-white" timbered buildings, & odd names for its streets,—"Dogpole St.," "Mardol," "Shoplatch," "Butcher Row," "Milk Street," "Pride Hill," and of course, its moat-like river has given it immense importance in all English wars against Wales, or civil wars. Its falling into the hands of the Roundheads—(about 1647, shortly after that visit of Charles I in the course of which he slept for three nights in my bed, in a room just across the hall from me, and wrote two letters, preserved in Evelyn's Diary, I am told, & there dated "Chetwynd"—who knows? perhaps in this very room under the towering shadow of a larch and a pine, or on my veranda, looking at the ancient peacock who struts about the lawn down there all day)—the fall, I say, of Shrewsbury was one of the greatest blows to the Monarchy.

I lunched with Burton Borough at 1³⁰ at the Shropshire Club, with his uncle Dick Jebb, who 6 weeks ago was in Canada, & could therefore give me the latest gossip of that rascal King[1]. The *Times* gives excellent extracts from the *Free Press* on one hand, & the Toronto *Globe* & Montreal *Star* on the other.

After lunch & a talk & smoke we drove 30 miles N.W. to "Newcastle under Lyme," where Borough, who is colonel or something of the Staffordshire yeomanry, had to take charge of a musketry parade. We had tea in the Mess Shed, then drove back past various hills, notably the Wrekin, a few minutes late for dinner...

[1] King: William Lyon Mackenzie King, then Canada's Prime Minister and leader of the Liberal party.

Sunday: 25th

Took a long walk over half the park after breakfast, went to
the Park Church at 11, had lunch at 1, & was taken up to
Miss Borough's bedroom to see her lovely pictures,—she talks
of "very cheap ones" at only two guineas, and complains of her
poverty that prohibits even a beautiful little ten-guinea
painting of Shepperson. "But then," she adds laughing, "you
can't expect much of a gallery from a girl who does it all out of
her dress allowance, and keeps two dogs and breeds Arab
horses from the same source, can you?" Shepperson—who died
two or 3 years ago—was a friend of the family, & has done a
lovely little painting of the drawing-room—the real drawing-
room, now closed down—which was a glorious room done in
gold & blue, with a magnificent ornamental ceiling. She
showed me also a lot that she has painted herself,—some very
good, tho' she never took a lesson,—& gave me this photo of
the house. She is awfully nice, sings most beautifully, & yet is
as simple & unspoiled as a dewy summer morning.

After dinner, we sat in the drawing-room listening to her
gramophone records of Caruso, & bagpipes, & English songs.
Lately she took a walking tour with Scottish friends in
Kircudbrightshire (pronounce "Ker-coo'-bry-shire") & did some
paintings & learned odd little things from Ross, an old
retainer who came up to her hostess's house at night to play
the bagpipes. She has inexhaustible knowledge of trees &
birds—some of which knowledge she promises to impart to me
tomorrow. On Thursday, alas! I go away.

Monday: 26th

(I write this on Tues. as I wait for eight o'clock to be announced by a bell that tolls across the Estate for the benefit of
the workmen: dinner is announced about five past eight, but I
am "dressed" & do not wish to go down to the drawing-room
just yet.)

On Monday I went with Burton Borough to see his show-
sheep, and saw not only them, but a more interesting thing

still, their Welsh shepherd. "Gude-mar-r-rnin' Surr-r," he says, touching his cap.

"Good morning, Llewellyn. I hear you have very good sheep this year for Newport show."

"Not so bad, Surr-r, not so ba-a-a-ad; ah'll git a bit a' warr-r-rk on 'um ag'in Thar-r-rsday, and they w-a-an't look so bad."

Here we go into a shed with half a dozen partitions, each containing a few sheep, & Llewellyn clambers over the hurdles, catches two immense woolly rams, like gigantic Jaeger caterpillars, around the neck—one hooked in each arm—and hauls them up for our inspection. "Ain't bad ones, Sur-r-r, is 'em? But if Lar-r-rd spares me an' I 'ave me 'ealth next year, I'll do better then nor now, so I wull, by God, Sur-r-r!" We yarn for nearly an hour with Llewellyn, who is one of the best drovers in the county, & has wonderful tales of sheep market dodges. But—enough of him for the present.

A long walk round the park after lunch with Cynthia, the younger daughter who has just gone down from Oxford, where we saw about a hundred fallow deer, & several herds, & countless rabbits, & in the lake a heron, Canada geese, a grebe & its nest, wild duck, etc. Then tennis with a New Zealander & Miss Shand. Dinner. Joseph Conrad & Ghost Stories, gossip with Cynthia & Borough. A whiskey & soda— not very pleasant; I shall not become an addict! and bed.

Tuesday: 27th

Cicero & a chat with Cynthia after breakfast. Then Mrs. Borough, who is the most handsome old lady I know, joined us & we visited the garden where flowers beyond number & fruits above measure—figs, melons, grapes, cherries, pears, tomatoes, marrows, apricots, nectarines—are ripening on the walls or in the hot-houses.

At 3³⁰ the car was ordered to take Mrs. B. & Cynthia & me to Eccleshall Castle where we had a very jolly tennis party at the Carters'. The castle was once the Palace of the Bippo [Bishop] of Lichfield, but His Lordship moved more to the centre of affairs in the last century. The present Bippo, by the way, excites great indignation all over England by his futile interference in the coal problem. Mrs. Borough read extracts from his pastoral letter in the Diocesan magazine at breakfast this morning, with appropriate comments of indignation. Burton came in a bit late, walked up to his mother and kissed her, nodded good morning to me, helped himself to eggs & bacon at the side table (as most English families do, I find) & sat down to listen.

"We are not carried away by the warm praise of some," (she reads) "nor by the exaggerated criticism of others who protest that we are exceeding our apostolic charge..." Burton leans forward angrily & cries "Well, what the bloody hell else is he doing, the old fool? Damn their interference." "That's what we all think," says Mrs. Borough indignantly, "it is damnable; it's too dreadful for anything."—This open language is not uncommon here; it has at least the merit of being open & straightforward. Mrs. Borough is a formidable lady, to evil doers, as this will show. She wanted stamps at Newport lately & asked at the post office counter for them; but when the attendant man pushed them across the counter six feet further along it than she was standing, she said "Please give them to me <u>here</u>." A mutter. An ill-tempered little poke that sent the stamps only a foot nearer to her. "I want the stamps given to me <u>here</u> please, where I stand. I may tell you that since you have been here you have been consistently offensive & disagreeable; it is to be hoped that your conduct will soon mend."—It did!

This afternoon, again, returning from the castle, the chauffeur Gates (a very poor driver, I admit: changing of gears is a difficult operation to him, & very badly performed) tried a long hill on top gear, with the natural result that the car all but stopped near the top. "Oh, Gates, oughtn't you to change gear?" cries Cynthia from the back (I was sitting in front with Gates). "Yes'um," says poor struggling Gates, but before he can well utter the words, an exasperated voice comes from Mrs. Borough. "Gates, you are a perfect fool. You ought to have changed <u>long</u> ago & not waited so stupidly till the car nearly stops. You <u>are</u> so tiresome." Here the despairing & perspiring Gates becomes doubly agitated, pushes all his feet down violently, shifts his gear lever with an ear-splitting crunching noise, and the engine stops!—It is started again & we bowl merrily homeward.

Mrs. Borough is very sweet, really, & of course the real noblewoman, imperious & exacting, but accomplished, kind, & the very soul of honour, & fairness, & truth. Meanness or petty feeling are unthinkable in her—She is the best type of the proverbial "Proud Salopians," referring with quiet self-possession & dignity to "the town people, just a little below one socially, you know,—the doctors & the solicitors, & so on; especially in these county towns where everyone knows everyone else." I raise a polite query about solicitors being excluded from the highest circles. "Well, you know Mr. West-gate—for instance in Shrewsbury one of the solicitors has a brother who is a shopkeeper..." and that is to be taken as conclusive! Yet I should never, and shall never, call Mrs. Borough a snob. She is no such thing.—Sorry that Miss Borough (Lysette) is not well today. She is so thoroughly sincere & jolly, intelligent yet not too clever, & so interested & interesting, in poetry & painting & animals that I should like to know her better. She is 29 or so, I think.

Thanks for Pater's copy of his letter to Picker: it is very good, I think (only Picker is not reverend.) He will answer it in confidence, I expect, so I shall not probably hear his reply...

AUTOBIOGRAPHY

When the summer vacation came, I arranged to take Dorothy to Paris to a hotel, and then to a *pension* in Tours where Mason Hammond and Donald McDougall, the blind Canadian, would also stay. There Dorothy and I would take French lessons, read our assigned books, and go to the Tours library. We also arranged a three day walking tour down the Loire and across the Inde to view some lovely châteaux like Azay-le-Rideau and Chenonceau, built across its rippling stream. I then took her back to England to sail home to Canada while I stayed with the ever-hospitable Hubert and Mona Watson in Salisbury, playing some tennis and getting on with my reluctant reading. Dorothy had fun on these vacations, but both of us were far too illiterate and unorganized to profit deeply by our opportunities. She, I think, had her juvenile heart in Winnipeg and the great Canadian West.

My two aunts, Kathleen who lived in a small house in Streatham and Beatrice in Salisbury, and my cousin Hubert were always hospitable, so I spent fragments of each vacation with them. Twice I stayed in France with an American widow, Mrs. McKaig, to tutor her two small boys, Jim and Clem, and to guard them from the alleged dangers of the surf at Biarritz.

One spring I also tutored a Canadian boy at Berne. Once I toured briefly with two Australians in a very small car. They were good historians, and I would have been wise to criss-cross Europe with them instead of roaming ignorantly alone, but I lacked the well-stocked mind from St. Mark's School and Harvard of Mason Hammond, or of Louis MacKay from Toronto or of Jack Knapton from British Columbia.

In much later married years, Sheila and I had excellent, well-planned vacations in Greece, Provence, around Assisi, and three times in the Mediterranean and in England. On all of these trips we benefitted from thoughtful organization and historical background reading. Looking back on my Oxford years and comparing them with the rich use made of them by Hammond and Knapton, I realize my lack of organization or background.

à 13 rue du Petit Pré
Tours, I. et L., France
19.ix.1926

My dear Mother

How well both you and Moll timed your letters, for both came by the first mail on the 14th [Bill's birthday]. It was all the nicer to get them together, because Dorothy had left me the 9th, and I was alone save for Hammond...

I got a card from the noble army of aunts, reinforced by the holy array of cousins, a week ago suggesting that I go to Brittany and enlist with them. But I'd rather carry on my own little guerilla warfare on my work and on French here, than lead that force into the most exciting battle for pleasure! Kathleen went home about the 13th, the others retreat either tomorrow (20th) or the 22nd. In point of fact, I should not have objected to a spell at the sea, for Brittany in September is getting cool, and is very invigorating, whereas the Loire is all very hot, and, like Oxford, a trifle relaxing: but I should only have had a week with them, and then have had either to remain alone, or go to England with them: the former would be the alternative I should have chosen in order to finish my work; and I decided that I could do better resting in the Touraine where I know excellent places, than going to Brittany on the mere chance of getting agreeable digs.

This week, accordingly, I am going to move, not out of Touraine, but twenty miles nearer Paris, to the dear village of Amboise: I have got a jolly old attic from which, by poking my head through the skylight, I can nod good morning across the great expanse of silver water and golden sand to the royal château of the last of the house of Capet:[1] and pretend to

myself that the old servant who ambles along that skyey parapet to the stables is the seneschal looking for the royal banners of Charles VIII and his queen Anne de Brétagne.[2] I am leaving Mlle. Sorbin chiefly because at Amboise I pay only 25 ₣ a day (90 cents) whereas here I pay 40 ₣ ($1.20), but partly because I want to be alone with my work for three weeks...

With love from Bill

[1] Capet or Capetians. The royal house of France which ruled continuously from 987 to 1328, when the throne passed to the house of Valois. After the fall of the monarchy in 1792, Louis XVI and Marie Antoinette were called Capets.

[2] Charles VIII (1470-1498), King of France 1483-98. He was married to Anne of Brittany in 1491 in the handsome castle at Langeais which Bill sketched "from a vineyard on the hills N. of the Loire — 7 am, 28.8.26." (Page 146.)

Balliol College, Oxford
Sunday, 17.x.1926

My dear Moll

After the long and cramping restriction of picture postcards, I am at last going to break out into a letter. After seven others, including a rather laborious one to Lady Clarendon, my ardour begins to fade a little: but I must thank you for the tie and sox—they were waiting for me when I arrived, through the perennial drizzle, late last Thursday night—and jolly glad I was to find them on my table to welcome me.

With Father's letter in my pocket, I made my congé to Amboise about noon last Monday, stopped for two hours to visit Blois, and reached Paris at 6... At the Gare d'Orsay I took a taxi to my hotel Lutèce, changed into dinner suit, and telephoned to the McKaig's hotel. Mrs. McKaig, I was told, was in the city, but not in the hotel at the moment. I scented a dinner, free and good, so took the autobus to the Hotel Savoy, rue de Rivoli, and asked for Mrs. McKaig. Up goes the bell-hop, while I wait in the lounge: in two minutes there is a

joyful howl, and I see Jim himself leaping at me —"Mr.
Westgate, Mr. Westgate!—Why aren't you at school?"—
"Twisted my knee: pretty lucky!" I had dinner there, then
went to the theatre with them, borrowed a novel by Radcliffe
Hall, took it to bed, and read until I woke up at noon next
day!... At 5 I bought my 3rd class ticket via Dieppe and
Newhaven to London.

A furious gale confounded sea & heaven (as Virgil would
say) when I embarked at midnight: I wished I were dead at
two minutes after midnight: I envied Job his happier lot at
ten after: I wished I were never born at quarter past. But I
arrived, had a bath at Newhaven at 8, went up to London
about 9. Then, after doing various odd jobs in London, came
here at 8^{30}... My new room is my own: very high up, near the
bathroom, looking into the quad and overlooking Trinity.

With love from Bill

— XIII —
"MINGLING WITH HUMANITY IS A NOBLE THING"
(November, 1926—January, 1927)

FROM DIARY LETTERS TO HIS FAMILY

Balliol College, Oxford

Monday, Nov. 15th, 1926

I read a paper on "Canadian Education" before Canon Streeter
and his "Jordan's Group" at Queen's College. The group (in
case I have not spoken of it before) is to meet in a barn or
farm house for a week at the end of next vac. (Jan. 13—20)
some way out of London, to read papers on subjects sacred &
profane in the evenings, & work & play during the days.
Someone asked if he might read a paper on "Conceptions of
the Devil." "Does that mean," asked Canon Streeter, "man's
conceptions of the Devil, or what the Devil thinks of himself?"

Tuesday, Nov. 16th

Read an essay (which I wrote in only two hours) on
"Character Drawing in Cicero's Orations" before Cyril this
evening, with three other men. Cyril is very amusing &
awfully good. In my essay, I had written, quite without
noticing the limerick jingle of it, something about "...the
unhappy old man of Panormus" (in Sicily). Just before I
uttered the words, the jingle caught my notice & I stopped
short in "when we turn to the character of the unhappy old
man..." "Good lord," I cried, "it goes like a limerick!" & I burst
out laughing, then began again "the unhappy old man of
Panormus..." Cyril simply exploded, & the other three after

him. The case of the said old man was that the infamous
governor Verres had put him in prison because of his wealth,
& had then appropriated all his possessions. So I finished it
off for Cyril—

The unhappy old man of Panormus
Whose riches & wealth were enormous
    Because of his kale
    was cast in gaol
Where he languished for years like a dormouse.

Thursday, Nov. 18th

After breakfast I met Dr. Luckham at Harold's digs, & drove
with him back to Salisbury, over the same road that I travelled alone on Uncle John's bicycle 31/2 years ago, when first I
visited Oxford. What memories!—Kathleen & Mona were alone
when I arrived, in the consulting room. Chatted for half an
hour till Hubert came in. Great surprise! Great chatterings!
Great jokings! After lunch I walked up to Castle Road, then
returned by the 3⁴⁰ train to Oxford. All look awfully well:
especially Mona, who seems prettier every time I see her. She
& H. are the perfect pair. Aunt B. is thin, but has good colour,
& Uncle John is irrepressible.

Having turned the evening into what is, in Oxford, considered good account, by turning incomprehensible old English
into unintelligible Greek prose, I am going to bed at 2 a.m.
Good morning!

Saturday, Nov. 20th

The Morrison Dinner: The "Morrison Fours" are the freshman
race which my crew won last year. Do you remember it? This
year an American named Mitchell from Virginia raced in the
finals against another American named Twitchell! At first it
was a dead heat. The second time, Mitchell beat Twitchell!

After dinner about 8 people came up to my room & sang
songs till 10³⁰. By that time the Hall was cleared & a band
was playing, presumably to allow us to dance. No one could

hear anything but the general uproar which made the Hall sway & rock, so we collected a few more spirits who wanted to sing, & retired to a room with a piano, where we sang till 12 o'c. When we got back to Hall, a joyful ring of people, hand in hand, were skipping & skirling round the Junior Dean, who was executing a Hieland [sic] fling in their midst. It closed very soon, & I went to bed.

Tuesday, Nov. 23rd

Tutorial with Cyril at 10³⁰. Very amusing lecture by Cyril on Lucretius at 11. Read Aristotle till 3, then went to the track for an hour. Coming back at 4 I asked Harman if it would be alright for me to "cut" Cyril's tutorial at 5³⁰ for which I ought to produce an essay. "No," replied Harman, "because mine is very short, and Paul Nairac has not got one at all. You'll have to do one." I did, in 1½ hours, & read it quite satisfactorily!

Went round to Christ Church to see a man at 9 o'c. Then got back to Balliol about 10. Climbed on to a scaffolding on St. Giles St. & rapped at what I took for MacKay's bedroom window. "Louis, Louis, open your window!" I saw, between the blind and the sill, a pair of pyjamas walking about, so I cried again "Louis!" The pyjamas stood still. "Louis!" They rose on their tip-toes. "Louis!" rap-rap-rap, I knocked the glass. The pyjamas trembled, then approached the window. The blind was pulled aside, & a poor, inoffensive terrified face appeared, speechless & gulping! "Oh, sorry; where is MacKay's room?" Gulps followed, but no voice. "Is it on this staircase?" "N-n-no, I d-d-don't think so." The poor wretch was almost gibbering, so I tried the windows, walking along the scaffolding—to the great interest of a cabby on the cabstand—till one gave to my push, & I climbed in. Goodnight! 11³⁰.

Thursday, Nov. 25th

S. Catherine's Day. The college are the guests of the Master & Fellows to a big dinner at night in Hall. I did <u>not</u> go. One Judge Kershaw, an old Balliol man, delivered the most boring speech ever snored through, even by Roy Wilson, who retailed the bloody details of the speech to me about 11 o'c. It was all about the Judge's hangings!.

"I was 28 before I hanged my first man!" (This is Wilson's report.) "It was in the Sahara. The man asked to be shot; I replied 'I haven't got a gun license, so you can't.' So we put him on a table, & tied a rope onto a tree & round his neck, & pulled away the table. But we forgot to tie his hands, so he climbed up the rope. He hid on the bough. My men got sticks. They poked him off it. He fell down & asked to be shot again…" I got a lot of work done & am glad I didn't hear the catalogue of criminals.

Saturday, Nov. 27th

Had half the Colonial Club team out in the Balliol Grounds for an American football practice, with a view to Monday's game. It will be great fun on Monday, "American Club" vs. "Colonial Club," but we shall be whitewashed in the half that's played under American rules, for among the Americans are Gates, a Princeton 1st eleven end, Pfair and Legendre, who were on the All-America first team, & Bond, on the All-America second team!

Gates came up to my room after tea, & gave us a practical demonstration, to the further detriment of my furniture. Last time he sat on a chair & broke it: this time we knocked down a picture & a plate of apples. The plate was broken, but it does not matter.

Monday, Nov. 29th

At 1³⁰ p.m. over a flickering fire & the relics of a cake, some banana skins, applecores, cigarette butts, a jug of mulled claret (empty, alas!) & empty coffee cups—the wreckage of a meeting of the Fallodon Club in my rooms—I pull my few remaining bones together to tell you about our American match.

They played two All-America first XI men, one All-America second XI man, one Princeton tackle, & one Swarthmore halfline man. We had two Canadians (I being one) & a pack of S. Africans & Australians who had never played American football, or seen it played. We lost the 1ˢᵗ half by 6 touchdowns—nil, & in the second half were drawn, nothing being scored. Two cracks on the head, a biff on the backbone, a thick lip, a torn ear, a stiff knee, a dislocated finger, & a twisted shoulder are all that I got out of the game, but I enjoyed it very much. The first half was American rugby; the second English.

Tuesday, Nov. 30ᵗʰ

I "Sconced" Freddy Wood at dinner tonight. If one speaks more than 3 foreign words, or uses bad language, or laughs coarsely, one of one's fellows writes on the menu card "Please sconce Mr. (Wood) for coarse laughter" and signs it. The Senior Scholar at table also signs it, & the menu is given to Mr. Wood in case he wishes to appeal to High Table. Wood appealed to High Table last night, i.e.: he wrote a Latin note to the Dean, denying my charge. The scout then took the menu card to the Dean, who read both my accusation & Freddy's appeal; & then wrote "Sconce granted." That means that Freddy is "Sconced," & is presented with a quart flagon of beer. He may either pass it round the table for everyone to drink, or drink it at one go himself. He drank it all himself, without taking the mug from his mouth, then handed the mug to me to certify that it was empty, which I did by turning it upside down on the table. Freddy had, in technical parlance, "floored his sconce," & I had to pay for it!

But a sconce does not end there. If I like, I can call for a second flagon; if I succeed in "flooring my sconce," then Freddy pays for both, or else calls for a third flagon: if he floors that too, I must pay, or floor a fourth, & so it goes on, whoever gives in paying for the total! He is going to try to make me floor one to get even with him tomorrow night, & continue the battle.

Wednesday, Dec. 1ˢᵗ

This is written on Thurs: for my sconce was produced
punctually at the dinner table last night, & by guzzling &
guzzling & guzzling steadily, without taking the pot from my
lips, I managed to "floor" the whole quart. But the excessive
drowsiness—to say nothing of the odd, chilly effect of a quart
of fresh-drawn beer within one's waistcoat,—was too great to
allow me to work: & after a short walk, I retired to bed about
9^{30}.

Wednesday, Dec. 8ᵗʰ

Went "beagling" today. Beagles are small hounds, white & tan,
with long tails that stick straight up when the pack is on the
scent. We (that is, Roy Wilson & I) got on the bus at Queen's,
on High Street, at 1^{20}, and rode out about 6 miles along the
road where Moll & I went one Sunday last year, till we came
to Oddington. There we all got out, & waited for the beagles to
arrive. Soon a green Ford drove up,—a sort of delivery van, &
the keeper jumped out in his snappy white breeks & green cap
and coat, ran round the back, unlocked the folding doors,
and—presto, out jumped thirty beagles!

Six Whips, all very smartly clad in white & green, and
bright brass buttons, started cracking whips, & led the pack
down the road, & into a field. In ten minutes the pack were
streaming all over two fields, sniffing the ground & running
here & there, while the Master blew his horn & the six Whips
cracked their lashes & encouraged the hounds. Twenty of us in
knots of two or three plodded along behind, commenting on
the day & the country & the prospects of a hare. It was very
pleasant: the land lay still & frosty all about us; the sun was a
red gilt disc in a wintry sky, and the sky itself was audibly
nippy & cold & tense. We plodded along over plow and fallow,
through turnips & meadows, crossing streams & clambering
over fences, intoxicated with the quiet beauty, which was all
the more pleasant for the suppressed yelping of an excited
beagle, and the distant cracking of a whip, and the odd hoarse
blast of the horn.

Not a hare was to be seen anywhere. Roy & I got lost in
an angry argument on Lucretius, & found when we came to,
that we were miles from anywhere & we couldn't join the pack
without wading a stream. So we plodded along by ourselves,
gossiping & joking & chaffing each other. We came to a hedge,
& climbed up the bank to get a view of the Whips,—their
white breeks were easy to see on the field,—but we could not
locate them except by the faint-blown echo of the Master's
horn. We saw a fox, however. Then we ambled back till we
found a tree overhanging the stream, climbed it, saw the pack,
jumped down to the other bank, and crossing two fields,
overtook it.

The sun was now low: it gilded & enamelled the western
clouds in a truly glorious fashion, & gave the sky that brilliant
light blue colour that is really heaven's blue. Looking through
the black tracery of a bare and lonely oak into that unfathom-
able blue one could see clearly, so it seemed, the lucid inter-
space of world and world, where dwelt the ancient gods—

> Where never creeps a cloud, or moves a wind,
> Nor ever falls the least white star of snow,
> Nor ever lowest roll of thunder moans,
> Nor ever sound of human sorrow mounts to mar
> Their everlasting calm!

The beagles were called up; wagging their tails & jumping
with delight at being abroad in the misty fields; "Not much
luck today, Sir" says Joe, the keeper. "No, we've drawn a
blank today, Joe." "Been a good day, though, Sir: quiet, like, &
still out here-ways, ain't it."

It was: marvelous as is Oxford, the country always beats
the town, & I walked as it were on air back to the village of
Oddington. The beagles went back into the van,—not without
yelpings, it must be confessed, and snarlings, & muffled yelps
& growls & squeals. We climbed into our bus, & drove a few
miles to the "Swan" at Islip, where a mighty tea was spread
for us, with piles of bread & jam & stacks of cake. At 5^{30} we

got back to Oxford, & washed & read for an hour or so till Hall...

Well, I must stop. Cyril is "at home" in his study, on Wednesday evenings, with a jug of lemonade, and after I have done a little more reading, I shall go to see him for a few minutes.

Monday, Dec. 13th

"Handshaking" at 9 o'c. Cyril was away, but when I sat down the Master took a sheet of paper & read: "Mr. Bailey says this of you, Westgate..." It was very nice in a way, but every report of my work nowadays seems to boil down to "honest but dull," or "industrious but slow." It gets very depressing: at times I could hang myself. But as an alternative to hanging, I think I'll take more sleep & harder exercise, work for less long spells, but with more vim, & mingle more with bright & cheerful folk. For the last fortnight I have been reading industriously—but slowly, and honestly—but dully: I shall have to get more of a "flair" to my work, or come a desperate cropper in Mods...

Tuesday, Dec. 14th

Read some of Rupert Brooke today. He served in Belgium & then in the Mediterranean, on the "British Mediterranean Expeditionary Force," and died in the Aegean. He is buried on the windy island of Skyros. He was 28 when he died (1915). Everyone knows some of his war-time sonnets like "Blow out, you bugles, over the rich dead," and

> If I should die, think only this of me;
> That there's some corner of a foreign field
> That is forever England.

—(in his case, windy Skyros): but a strange thing called "The Great Lover" has good lines for Shotover Hill,—in fact, Ruth mentioned the "High Places" when we paused on the brow of Shotover, & spoke of Rupert Brooke:

"moist black earthen mould...and high places; footprints in the dew; and oaks."

These, and many other things, are what Brooke, "the Great Lover," says that he loves: his enumeration, queerly enough, does not mention horses, or dogs, or birds; in fact, nothing more animate than flowers and clouds! Whereas I would sell my soul—or anyway a good lot—if I could have a horse of my own. First a horse, and then if I can afford it,—or her?—a wife.

Wednesday, Dec 15th

Left Oxford at 12^{56} and got to Newport at 6^{30}, but to my horror my trunk had not been taken off the train & I was stranded without any evening clothes! I was met by Gates, the old groom, in a small car, & driving up to Chetwynd Park, found Mrs. Borough there and excused myself for not having dinner clothes.

Tomorrow night we are to drive about 20 miles to Stafford, for the County Ball at 9^{30}, and on Friday we are going to the North Staffordshire Hunt Ball.

Thursday, Dec. 16th

The Ball: Dinner at 7^{15}, then into the two cars at 8^{15} and away to Stafford. About 340 people were at the County Hall, the girls (& old women!) in brilliant dresses, & the men in the smartest of "tails" or—sight for the Gods!—in long-tailed scarlet [or "pink" in hunting circles] hunting coats.

The Borough party girls (i.e. Miss Lysette, Miss Cynthia, & a visitor, Miss Something) were rather a trial in the actual dancing; they are so lumpy & ponderous; and the younger (Cynthia) is of the fearfully mannish Queen-Victoria type that insisted on leading me in the dance till I seized her like a vice & fairly squelched her into shape. Ah me! there were such perfectly divine people there,—an awfully pretty girl with reddish hair, who came with a party of people in hunting coats,—and I was trundling the Boroughs round the room.

We got back about 4 o'c.

Friday, Dec 17th

The North Staffordshire Hunt Ball: was held at a lovely house called "Maer," and was more brilliant a show than last night: for half of the men wore red coats, & the house was so beautiful that everybody was much more friendly & jolly than last night. A lot of people whom I met in the summer at tennis were there...

It was perfectly jolly, & I could not credit my partner when she told me it was a quarter to four. A little later we stopped, with "John Peel" & "Lang Syne," & "God Save the King," & by 5 we were home. I hear the wakeful cock now as I write this about 5^{30}.

Saturday, Dec. 18th

I continue this at 5^{30} Sat. morning for I want to post it from Shropshire.

Linzee & I travel up to London tomorrow morning (I mean <u>this</u> morning (Sat.) & I go to Aunt K's for tea. On Tues. 21st I meet Dorothy at Streatham, & we stay there for Christmas, & until Dec. 29th.

Then to Lady Drury's for a week. Then Jan 5th D. goes to Cotteridge, to Mrs. McLaughlin, & I to Redhill, or Salisbury, or Streatham again: & eventually about Jan 21 back to Oxford.

I do want to get my Mods work well in hand this vac. and I hope you will remember me more particularly in respect of my reading, when you think of me in prayer. I cannot make half the progress that I expect to do, & get desperately discouraged about the whole business occasionally, so if I know that you are also thinking of me & wrestling for me, so to speak, I may get on better. Now—unless the breakfast gong interrupt me in my writing! I must get into bed.

Duchess of Connaught Memorial Hostel
14 Bedford Place, London W.C. 1

Monday, Jan. 10th, 1927

It is extraordinary how kind Lady Drury was to us [Bill &
Dorothy]. She arranged that we should go to four dances, and
we went to a fifth. For all these, a lordly limousine from the
village drove round for us two, & we kept our man waiting till
12 or 1...She gave instructions at the Golf course that I was to
play whenever I liked & every charge was to be made against
her, not excluding lessons (if I had wanted them) with the pro.
She let me invite Ross over to lunch twice, & Helen Groves &
Ross once. Though we came long after Christmas (the 29th of
Dec.) she gave me a lovely fur-lined pair of gloves for a present, and Dorothy was presented with lovely green material
which Emmeny, Lady Drury's maid, made up into an awfully
pretty dress for her...

No wonder, as I stewed over Aristotle in the Library all
day, my mind flew off to the happy days & nights of last week;
the golf with Enid, and the bridge, or the rides of "Ethelred,"
the motorbike, with Ross; or the lovely waltzes on the last
night at the Robson's party with Enid, who dances most exquisitely (and I am at my best in a waltz). Ho! Ho! A weary
sigh, and a long goodbye, and another few chapters of
Aristotle.

What if I don't get a 2nd in Mods? The memory of those
jolly days & nights, & the thought of seeing Ross & Enid again,
& all the rest of them, when I go down to my digs in the farm
in the summer outweighs a first! Oh, most easily!

I'll work, of course: for after 25 I don't expect to get much
idle pleasure, or indulge in dances & such gaiety. I am far
from absorbing myself in them. I don't cry "Eat, drink & be
merry, for tomorrow we die," nor do I moan—

Fill the can & fill the cup.
   All the weary ways of men
Are but dust that rises up
   And is lightly laid again.

But this mingling with humanity is a noble thing, and it will help me five hundred times better to rule a class, or a congregation, or a consular office (whatever it may be I decide to rule!) than the lame-dog "first" that I might have got by burying myself in a lonely library.

Ten strikes. I must to bed in an hour, so goodnight, and much love to you all.

"*TOMORROW TO FRESH FIELDS*"
(*March—April, 1927*)

My dear Father

I am rather relaxing my efforts now, in view of examinations this week. The term has been (so far) very pleasant, and very strenuous: a good deal of the programme that I set myself has been accomplished, and what failed to get done is compensated by the experience I got stroking the Second Togger[1].

The training was a splendid thing physically, & did not much interfere with work. As for Togger Week, when we had a run & cold shower at 7^{30}, and went out to breakfasts (or gave breakfasts among ourselves) from 8^{30} to 9^{30}, and rowed a race every afternoon, & went out to dinners—that also was very jolly, and kept me in great spirits, tho' I was too exhausted in the evenings to do much work.

Now comes the final week. I feel very fit, and, on the whole, wish the wretched examinations would hurry up. My work is fairly well in hand. We have (a) to translate four authors, Homer, Virgil, Cicero, Demosthenes. I've read all Homer & all the prescribed Cicero, half Virgil, and 3/4 Demosthenes, so in those 4 papers I expect to get one or two "alphas" and nothing lower than "β." Next (b) we have to prepare very carefully four other books, (with translation and critical notes, history of extant MSS, and so forth). These books are (in my selection) Thucydides, Lucretius, Horace , and Greek Dramatists (= 4 Greek plays of Aeschyles, Sophocles &

Euripides). In this department I hope to get an "alpha" for the Dramatists, (whom I have done with desperate efforts at memory) and for Lucretius. Horace & Thucydides will disappoint me bitterly if they fail to give me β^+. Thirdly (c) we have Greek prose composition & Latin prose composition, (d) a general essay paper, and (e) a Special subject, in which my option is Aristotle's "Art of Poetry" with the history of the Greek drama. Perhaps (d) and (e) will gain me two more alphas, so that I may get 6 alphas out of my 12 papers: I don't think it's possible for me to get more than 6, (while it won't be difficult to get considerably less than 6!): and as it requires a minimum of 7 alphas to win First Class Standing, I can't in my most sanguine moments credit myself with more than a Second.

This letter ought to be a "Togger Number:" after all, what are Honour Mods. compared with Toggers, when Balliol I are second on the River, and Balliol II are 9th and so ten places higher than any other college's II togger in the varsity? What if I do go down despondently to the "Examination Schools" in High Street next Thursday, wondering what on earth I've got to say to Lachmann's proposed emendation for "proporro" in line 1001 of Book V of Lucretius? I remember that last Thursday we got into a perfectly strange eight, borrowed from Oriel barge, and with cheers and the firing of pistols, paddled down from the Balliol raft to Iffley Lock, and took up our position on the river just a length and a half ahead of Brasenose I crew.

The critics had prophesied that Brasenose would go up a place every night, and they smiled serenely at us—"a smile serene and high"—as they swung past us, and turned a little below us, just as the 5 minute gun went off. Those terrible 5 minutes! Supporters on the bank make fatuous remarks, and one replies with a sickly smile & looks at his oar, & feels the straps on the stretcher and—"Two minutes gone!" I turn to number 7 and remark that the water is jolly good for rowing and—"Three minutes gone!" The starter of our boat gets his boat hook in my rigger, and pushes us out a little way, then says "Sweaters off, gentlemen, please." We pull them over our heads, and are wrestling with them when there's a mighty BANG!—the minute gun. Sweaters are pulled off and tossed into the punt in which the starter stands with his boat hook. "Quarter gone!" He pushes us out gently, calling now and again "Bow & Two, lightly," then again "Lightly, Bow & Two!" —Our time-keeper, watch in hand (just out of the right corner of my eye I can see him on the tow path) cries "Half Gone!" The boat hook is straining at my rudder, & bending as the high flood wants to carry us on its broad surface down the channel.

"Hold her up again, Bow Two; lightly,"

That's a bit better, I feel, & press my feet on the stretcher, and put my oar in position, & feather it once or twice to get the feel & balance of it.

"Bow & Two, again" says the starter.

—"Three quarters gone!" cries time-keeper.

—"Drop the bung, sir!" cries starter, "Bow, very lightly!"

"Ten!—nine!—eight! seven! six!" cries time-keeper.

"Bow & Two!"—the starter's voice.

"—five!—four! three! two! one! (a pause like an aeon) then
        BANG!

We leap on our stretchers & go hard back: first stroke, long; second stroke, fast & furious; third is long; fourth you swing out to it. Well done boys!! Reach out for it! <u>Harder</u> back! <u>Harder</u> back! <u>Harder</u> back & slowly forward. <u>Harder</u> back & slow-ow-owly forward!

Well rowed, Balliol! Well rowed, boys! Well rowed! Now, then, you're going up! You're going up! up! up! up! Give her ten, now! 1—2—3—4—5—6—7—8—9—10. Another 10! leap on those stretchers! Time! Time! Time! Watch the time in the bows! You're late, Four, watch it Four! You're going up! You're going up!

These are the cries from the tow path, and also from our cox who sits just at my feet & steers like a wizard. His name is Henry Pelham. It seems we've been rowing for eternity, yet we've not got to Weir's Bridge yet. Oh thank God! here's Weir's Bridge, & there's where our first crew started. The Bargee gives us a hail as we plough by him; good old Robinson! blessings on your hearty shout. I hear him: then my right eye catches sight of him, kneeling in the punt fast by the bank, his hands trumpeting his mouth & sending us a stentorian roar "Come on boys! Come on boys! You're goin' up! up! up! Legs! legs! legs! legs! Well rowed, sir!"

So we sweat past the last punt, past the free ferry, going well. But as we swing out into the stream to get the current for the Gut, I see Brasenose boat has crept up on us half a length, and is now only one length behind us.

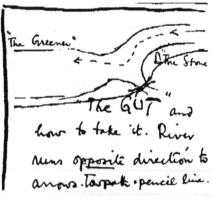

"Henry, give her ten!" "Give her ten!" yells Henry, "1—2—3—4—5 … 10—Well rowed boys! Steady, keep on your feet through the Gut! Harder back!" But Brasenose also gave her 10. And they are ten pounds heavier each man than we are, and are creeping up.

A gun is fired from the bank—that means they are less than a length away. But Henry steers a good course through the Gut, & they do a bad one, rather, so we gain, ever so little, and emerge from the willows to "the Greener." Here Bevan & Colman are ready to race along the bank & yell at us.

That's Bevan's colossal bellow "Balliol, Balliol! Oh, well rowed, you're going up, boys!," and that's Colman "Harder back, boys! Tear it back! Hell for leather, row like tigers!" But Brasenose get up to half a length, and BANG—BANG, two guns. I see their stroke get faster! "Very well, you brutes, I can do that too! and I tell Henry to give her ten, then raise the stroke and we gain again, but—oh so little! A mere yard, and we've only just got on to "the Greener." Three quarters of a mile to go still before we can get safe. Can we hold out?

"Steady! Steady! hands away faster! faster yet! Slowly forward and <u>rip</u> it back.That's the way! Now give her ten again!" But while Bevan & Colman imprecate us from the bank, Brasenose have come up on us again! Oh, damn the boat, how she rolls! Brasenose are up to two yards of our rudder, and each stroke gains them inches: we are done, done, done!

"Henry, a good ten."

The stroke has been 38: it goes up to 42 for ten strokes. "Another ten." It stays at 42. "Another ten." Brasenose are not any nearer, but how long can our eight men row at 42 to the minute? It drops a fraction, just two strokes, perhaps, and Brasenose forge nearer. "BANG—BANG—BANG" Three guns! That means "Go all out. You're within an ace of bumping,'" and Brasenose fairly bat the water. How I raised the stroke then, I can't conceive: but we kept our meager four or five feet to the New Cutting. There you cross to the other bank, and skillful coxing gained us perhaps two yards.

Now for the last stretch, 300 yards past all the barges. Mitchell is on the path with a megaphone; Bevan & Colman are left behind. "Well rowed, Balliol keep it up, stroke! Now give her ten."

Oh, these heart-breaking "tens." For the tenth time we give her ten! Again, ten! again! Bring her in, now boys. A hundred yards to go: well rowed, well rowed, well rowed Balliol! Oh joy, B.N-C (= Brasenose) are more exhausted than we are, & their nose drops behind a foot, two feet, a yard, two yards—Hurray! Hurray! They're dying! here's St John's Barge,

here's Balliol Barge, here's Tim's Barge, here—hurray!—is the
Safety post. B.N-C are five yards astern. Well rowed, second
togger! Well rowed, sir!

So Toggers are over for another year. On two days we got
bumped, but on the other four we "rowed over," and so are
still the only II boat in the First Division.

There was a great dinner that evening and many toasts:
next day there was a great luncheon at "the Grid," with few
toasts but much champagne and hilarity. Now the somber
week before Mods.

It's not going to be so very somber, however, for on
Tuesday I'm going down to Tenterden with Philoctetes[3] (that's
our motorbike, Wood's and mine) & I shall stay overnight with
Lady Drury, & perhaps play golf with Enid...

Your affectionate son,
Bill

---

[1] "Togger" or "torpids" are the names for inter-college boat races held
in February at Oxford. A "togger" is the name of a special kind of boat.

[2] Bumping: Because the Thames River is too narrow for the boats of all
the colleges to start abreast, each is assigned a starting place along the
bank derived from the college's position at the end of the previous year.
At the starting gun, each boat tries to overtake and bump the stern of
the boat ahead. When this happens, both boats retire to the bank and
reverse their starting positions the following day. This goes on for six
days of racing. If a boat achieves "four bumps," each member receives
his own oar, with the college crest and all their names, positions and
weights carefully painted on its blade. Bill's oar from "Eights Week" in
May, 1927 has followed us through all our moves and now rests on the
wall of our guest cottage. —SMW

[3] Philoctetes: Keeper of Hercules' bow and poisoned arrows, who had
a reputation for being very vocal. On the way to the Trojan Wars he
was bitten on the foot by a snake, causing a wound which emitted
strong odors.

Balliol College, Oxford
Sunday, March 13th, 1927

My dear Father

I have had rare doings since last Sunday and have enjoyed them very well. On Monday I got on our motorbike at 4³⁰ (having finished my Thucydides at 4) and started for Tenterden in Kent; but I hadna' gone a mile, a mile, a mile but barely—well 7 or 8 I suppose, when the drive belt broke, and I was compelled to push the beast two miles to get it mended. That done, I progressed to the first little pub, ordered tea and eggs, and dozed comfortably by the fire till 7. The village elders then began to assemble for their vespertine solemnities, and I decided to push on. First night, hotel near Henley.

On Tuesday I arose at 7, gave the kick-starter its first kick at 7¹⁵ and its two hundredth at 7⁴⁵. Without stopping for anything save petrol, and to send an apologetic telegram to the Butlers,—without stopping even for flooded roads near Eton & Windsor, nor for the absurd silk "shiners" in which Etonians conceal their cerebral lack of lustre, I pushed on to Tenterden & lunched at Chestnut House at 2³⁰...

At Chestnut House I distinguished myself by falling asleep while Enid and her mother were talking to me! They have such nice, soft voices. I distinguished myself two days ago, too, by doing the same thing in an exam on Greek unseens,—but I'm coming to that. Well, dinner was very, very, very pleasant, and Mr. Butler & I afterwards compared— though each protested that there could not really be any comparison at all—Cambridge of the 'nineties with Oxford of the 'twenties. At nine o'clock I said I must go. I hated to go. The fire was red and inviting and my chair was incredibly comfortable and Mr. Butler got quite witty and Mrs. Butler said there was a spare bed ready and Enid laughed and said that I could not get put up at that hour anywhere on the road. I didn't propose to put up on the road. I was going to an hotel: well, they'd all be shut. She was nearly right, for when I got to Maidstone at 11³⁰ I had a hard job to find a bed; but I djdn't know that then, so at 9^{15} I gave Philoctetes his first kick, and at 9^{30} his thirtieth, said goodbye to Enid, and struck north for London...

Exams began next morning, with Latin Prose: I did a fair one, I believe. In the afternoon, Virgil pleased me, Cicero made me grind my teeth. The Archangel Gabriel would have ground teeth, if he'd read 16 of the 19 proscribed orations during his last summer vac. and then found that 2 of the 3 questions given us were from the 3 he'd left unread! On Friday morning we had Homer & Demosthenes: I read the Odyssey in January, & got it all cold; the Iliad I conjectured more or less accurately. Demosthenes bored me, but I treated him with studied courtesy till 12^{30}.

After lunch I had two unseens, verse from Apollonius Rhodius, prose from Aeschines. I copied them out roughly on loose paper, then folded my hands on the table, and laid my head upon them and slumbered like a child for quarter of an hour. Greatly refreshed, I awoke at 4 o'c. and copied the translation into my examination booklet. If I don't get an alpha on that paper I shall be vexed. Yesterday morning we had Greek Prose, which I expected to be my Waterloo. I may have got a β^+ on it: in the afternoon we wrote on four Greek tragedies. I got all the translation & most of the "gobbets," i.e. grammatical cruxes and points of MSS corruption and variant readings. The worst papers are now passed. *Laus deo.* I'm now going to lunch with Picker, alias Arthur Pickard-Cambridge. He has just bought a car, so that I hope the conversation can be steered onto the subjects of gears and spark plugs. My motorcycle, by the way, I surnamed Philoctetes because it emits noisome odors and utters cries which not only preclude the possibility of religious ceremony in the neighborhood, but positively encourage anti-religious demonstration. See the play of Sophocles, passim.

With much love from Bill

Royal Colonial Institute
London, W.C.2
Wednesday, March 23, 1927

My dear People

The epistolary Sabbath passed without its due epistle, &
here is Wednesday upon me with my debt still to pay. I'm still
dazed after Mods., hardly able to realize how free I am, & sur-
feiting on the long verboten pleasures of theatres & dancing.

What about the night, Der Nacht (if that is any language
at all?), the dinner at Pitt House, and the great dance? Well,
that story must wait a minute.

Last Thursday night, on the eve of my last examination,
Picker & Cyril gave a dinner party to the Mods. men: all went
very nicely, especially for me, because I sat in the middle of
the table between two hearty people who talked of conven-
iently low-brow things like soccer and motors, and so had the
great, and rarely-given to mortals to enjoy, pleasure of seeing
my friends at one end of the table labouring to amuse Picker,
and my friends at the other end smiling statuesquely from the
soup course to the savoury at Cyril's well-matured jokes, while
I myself was outside both danger zones.

The exams ended rather dismally, but we had a Boat
Club dinner on the evening of the last exam, which gilded the
thick Lucretian darkness of the day, and the night proved
more bright than the day; for in the quad after dinner we had
a mild fight with Trinity (Trinity adjoins Balliol) and Trinity
threw fireworks at us. One fell at my feet & fizzed for a
moment. I seized it to throw it away, but it exploded in my
hand & tho' it only singed my skin, it blew away half my shirt
cuff, and one section of the famous Woolworth Kum-apart cuff
links which I purloined from Father two years ago. I am sorry
about the Missing Link.

Next day, I had Cyril Bailey as my guest at lunch, and
Maurice Hutton and B.J.F. Wright (whose father is Primate of
Australia). Cyril told "a good one" about misprints that
appeared in the Master's translation of Plato's Republic,—in
the proofs, that is. The context is a dialogue and Socrates

says: "The avaricious mind, it seems to me, is never content with any fortune, but is ever restless, pursuing now one profession and now another, as this or that appears to it to be more conducive to itches." Phaedo replies: "You're tight, Socrates!" The -R- was very conspicuous by its absence!

On Sat. evening I dined with Dr. & Mrs. Abbott-Smith at their hotel, and gave them Mother's kind messages: I read the words which she wrote "you will appreciate his scholarliness more than when you were younger," to Mrs. Abbott-Smith's intense pleasure! I talked for an hour after dinner to the Canon & then went for a walk with him, as Father & I occasionally did at home. They could not lunch with me on Monday, so I asked them to breakfast at 9, and trusted to Providence that the Junior Dean would allow me to give a breakfast party. Leaving them, I called at Queen's College to invite Canon Streeter of Queen's—an eminent but very amusing & (I believe) rather heretical theologian—as well. Most luckily, as it turned out, he was away for the weekend.

Next morning at 8^{30} I went down to the bathroom & met the Junior Dean & hailed him, and spake a word (as Homer would say) and named it forth: "Hail, noble Rodger, king of men, who marshallest the ranks of our fair-haired youths, and art umpire at many a contest where men kick with their feet the leathern ball that is cunningly fashioned in the semblance and image of an egg, wherewith the fair-haired youths disport themselves until what time Orion sinks beneath the dim horizon and the rainy Pleiades bring sickness to mortal men (all this has nothing to do with the point of the matter: it is Homeric) —may I give breakfast in my rooms this dawn, ere the dews have fled away, to a wandering priest who comes from beyond the Gates of Herakles, and the land of the Phæacians, and the circling stream of Oceanus, on a well-benched ship, with his white-armed lady by his side, even Jemima, the daughter of great-hearted Eëtion and fair-girdled Areté, who dwelt in woody Labrador, by the yellow streams of the river St. Lawrence?"

"No," said the Dean, "it's against the rules: you can't give breakfast parties in Balliol except on Sundays."

At that my flabber gasted: but concealing my emotions I sprinted in my dressing gown across the road to the Randolf Hotel & ordered breakfast for three to be sent up to my rooms on a tray at 9.

I then had a shower & got on with my dressing and was at the collar-and-tie business when steps were heard on the staircase. The scout who came flying to Horatius & the conscript fathers, all wild with haste & fear, from the face of Lars Porsena, had no worse news for the Great City than had this scout for the Great Man. "Sorry, sir. Randolf Hotel has sent word that it don't send out breakfasts any more." The clock struck a quarter to nine.—

Briefly, I put on a kettle to boil: I sprinted down the Giles and bought eggs, butter & bread: I sprinted down "the Corn" & bought egg-cups: I sprinted to the stores & got marmalade: I sprinted to the kitchen & got cream and to Hall & got cutlery, & at 9^{10} the guests arrived, & at 9^{15} we had breakfast!

I lunched with Wallace Johnston (of Winnipeg) at Brasenose College, & dined [in London] with the Countess of Clarendon on my right, and Miss Beardmore of Toronto on my left, with Lord Hyde in the starboard offing and Lady Joan Villers on the port bow: the noble earl was a point or two to starboard, ahead of my bows. It was a very jolly meal; it began at 8^{30} and went on till a quarter after 10. Then Lady Clarendon rose & led the damsels forth, while we passed the care-dispelling bottle round the table, from the noble Earl to Christopher Morrison (a friend of mine from Trinity, Toronto), from Chris to Leif Egeland, Egeland to MacDougall (the blind one), MacDougall to me, me to George Hyde, Hyde to Wallace Johnston, Johnston to the noble Earl all over again. We had a long discussion on riding, and the French, Italian & English jumping seats, until 11 o'c; then we met the damsels, & put on our opera hats and dark coats (nearly all borrowed) & motored from Hampstead to S. James' Square.

The dance was splendid. The Prince had come & gone
again when we arrived (at the 6th dance, rather late) but I met
Baldwin, & saw Amery & John Buchan and a quaint dear old
lady in a silvery grey crinoline! Her hair was done in a tower
over her head, & heavily powdered (or so it looked), & she
carried a little fan & bobbed & danced with a little grey old
man as tho' "increasing years," as Mother calls them, were a
direct advantage in waltzing & a distinct aid in the
Charleston.

I enjoyed the dance vastly more than last year, pleasant
as it was then: for I knew Lady Clarendon quite well, & Lady
Joan, & one Miss White who was there last year as well: but
most of my dances were with one called, for convenience,
Diana the Goof. It sounded like that, anyway, when Lady
Clarendon introduced us before dinner.

She is Irish, & dances very well, & as I found out later, is
a daughter of General Goff, V.C., who was killed in the war.
But my name fits her very well. (I don't mean that she has
consented to adopt my surname; only that Diana the Goof is
very appropriate.) She was going to drive me home, but I had
to go with MacDougall: in gratitude, however, to her for the
kind thought, I'm going to burst into song about her:

> Diana the Goddess gave proof,
> When she hunted the beasts on the hoof,
>   That her strength was immense:
>   But she's a past tense
> When compared with Diana the Goof.

Cease, Muses, cease your Pierian lay: we parted at 2³⁰, the
Clarendons for Hampstead in preparation for an early start
next morning for Venice, others for their respective beds, the
Goof to Regent's Park, and melancholy us to our diggings.

I am going to Redhill for 10 days tomorrow, to be joined
by Dorothy on the 31st. About the 5th of April we'll go off to
Salisbury, and on the 20th, when Wood delivers Philoctetes

over to me again, I hope we'll both go down, with the sidecar, to Lady Drury's for three days.

With much love to you all, from the liberated pedant,

Bill

Trusloe Manor,
Avebury, Marlborough
Easter Day [April 17, 1927]

My Dear Westgate:

I'm afraid that the Mods. result will be a blow to you and I am very sorry about it. I think that the truth is that you have not got quite the faculty of a good examinee: you get too much interested in some parts of your work and in some parts of a paper, when you are doing it & the consequence is that the whole suffers. But I hope it won't worry or depress you too much. Much more important than the class is what you really got out of the work you have done and I am quite sure that Mods. has given you much which will be a permanent possession—some of the authors and much of the archaeological side of Greek life. When you come to Greats you must try and tie your errant mind down a little tighter to the immediate point.

Meanwhile I hope you are having good weather in a good place. Here it has been lovely in spite of a good deal of cold wind & some days of rain like that when you were here.

Yours very sincerely,

Cyril Bailey

at Chestnut House
Tenterden, Kent
21.iv.1927

My dearest Father

You will be sorry to hear that I was put in the third class in Honour Moderations. Mona read the news to me last Monday, and a letter from Cyril next day as I was leaving Salisbury confirmed it. I enclose his letter.

What am I to do about it? There's nothing to do about Mods. itself,—that's flat. What am I to do, though, about the future in general, and about Greats in particular? Shall I, for the next two years, eschew dancing & athletics & irrelevant work and amusement? For the first, namely dancing, I am tempted to foreswear it forever: for I was so depressed on Tuesday night at the dance at Sir Auckland Geddes, even (or rather, "particularly") in Enid's company, that I was as glum as an oyster. For the second, namely athletics, I propose to hang up my golf clubs permanently, & preserve only my tennis racket, skates, running shoes and rowing togs. By irrelevant work, I mean sketching & astronomy, and by amusements, bridge & billiards & clubs of the idler sort.

Well, assume that I do cut all this out: will my work improve? It will have more time devoted to it, in the first place, and in the second, it will be more in the limelight of my thoughts. But neither of these advantages will help me very much, for they do not touch the root of my evil, which is this: that my mind is much too lethargic and wandering in its operation ever to achieve much. Could I but get a good cutting edge upon it and then instil some "drive" into it, I should do well.

I will never believe that I am a dullard. I will never believe that I am devoid of animus and manly power of will. Consequently I will never believe that I am condemned by nature to have an edgeless mind and an errant, feeble "drive." The metal I inherited from you and Mother is good, and the vigour (at times) that should make it vibrate, manifests itself in some constructive efforts that I occasionally make. So I must try to "tighten down" by strict discipline the wandering, unstable will, and to sharpen by strict constructive labour the rusting metal of my mind, and so destroy the film and corrosion that long absence of vigorous use have allowed to generate.

It is not often that I write to you thus introspectively. This letter is an attempt to put into black & white the sore thoughts of the last few days. I hope the result of writing them out will be to make me follow their guidance better.

I have had a most happy time here on the whole. On Tuesday I arrived, & after dinner went with Enid to a dance at Sir Auckland & Lady Geddes' house. Alexander, Ross & Peggy Geddes are awfully jolly & I might have enjoyed the dance in better spirits. I had an interesting talk during two dances with Sir Auckland, who is prepared with good evidence to substantiate his condemnation of "the Y.M.C.A. type of American missionary."

On Wednesday morning I read Shakespeare in the garden. In the afternoon we motored to Littlestone, near Rye, for a picnic, & when Enid went to a rehearsal of "The Sport of Kings," by Ian Hay, I read more Shakespeare at home.

Today I played 9 holes with Enid & her young cousin Dudley. After lunch—Sir Auckland & Lady G. were expected, but failed to appear—we played a short foursome with one Lade & Helen Groves, then in the club house played an hour's bridge. The Geddes came to tea with us, & Lade & Helen; & at tea Lady Geddes suggested that in place of playing more bridge we all drive over to their tennis court. Which forthwith we did, & played two sets. In the second, I stood out, & got Davy Geddes, 10, to show me round the grounds, which Sir Auckland has laid out & converted, in three or four years, from bare country to orchards, lawns, rockeries & gardens.

After supper we drove to Enid's rehearsal, where Dudley & I & Faith (another cousin, 14) worked gramophones to represent "confused noise without," & saw "The Sport of Kings." Enid is awfully good & has been commended by Ellen Terry.

Here I must end. Tomorrow, Friday morning I return to Oxford to lead, I hope, a wiser & more vigorous & more purposive life. I am sorry for the family's sake to have done no better in Mods., but I have done with them now. "Tomorrow to fresh fields."

Your son,

Bill

SMW

While Bill was disappointed with his "Third in Mods," it could have been worse—there are four classes of Mods. His immediate future included one more year at Balliol similar to the first two. In addition, there were two weeks of training at a cavalry camp and rowing in the Torpids in the Balliol First Eight. The crew made "four bumps" and consequently won their oars.

In the winter of 1927-28, Bill was a member of the Oxford University ice hockey team which played against Cambridge in a series of competitions throughout Europe. In the summer of 1928 he was a member of the Balliol crew that was invited by Prince Olaf of Norway to take part in the Oslo Regatta.

The problem of the fourth year at Oxford, for which the Rhodes Trust does not provide, was solved when the University of Western Ontario in London, Ontario, offered him a position to teach Classics for two years while an instructor was on leave of absence.

He was also invited to be Dean of Residence at Huron Theological College at the same university, which provided him with both rooms and meals. So for two years Bill taught at Western and studied by himself in preparation for his Oxford examinations. It was during this period that Bill and I met.

In June of 1930 he returned to Oxford, took the examinations and obtained a B.A. in Classics, formally called "Literae Humaniores," or more popularly known as "Greats." As he had taken an extra year to do this, he was not classed for Honours. Each paper was rated alpha, beta, gamma or delta by two examiners separately; in Bill's case in none did they agree! He then toured with the Balliol Players in *Rhesus* by Euripides and made a personal tour of the Roman sites of England.

In the fall of 1930 he joined the faculty of Harvard University as an Instructor in Classics, proctor and student advisor. Here he organized a club of some twenty Latin teachers from Massachusetts schools who met for lunch and mutual stimulation. He gave several speeches at preparatory schools and later addressed the annual meetings of both the American Philological Association and the Classical Association of New England. He was also induced to work for a Ph.D. at Harvard, which he received in 1935.

During the summer of 1932 Bill joined his father on an expedition to northern Saskatchewan to inspect Indian schools, travelling by truck, horse and canoe. They were pleased that one of the men on the team was an Indian whose life Rex had saved by amputating his gangrenous arm several years before.

Bill and I were married in the summer of 1934 and together we explored the then little-travelled and beloved Greece. We were fortunate during other summers to visit many more Mediterranean ports and countries. On one of these trips, Bill left me in Venice while he made a hurried journey to the Vatican Library in search of Valla's original and yet undiscovered translation of Thucydides. After many later versions were produced by the librarian, the earliest copy, signed in Valla's own hand, finally appeared just as Bill had to leave to catch his train back to Venice.

He boarded the train in some excitement, but when the conductor came around he was told that his ticket was one-way, not round-trip, and was thrown off the train at the next stop. He did not have enough money to purchase another ticket, and so proceeded with a series of embarkations and throwings off until he finally reached Venice, to the great relief of his wife.

For nine years (1935-1944) Bill taught Latin and Ancient History at Phillips Academy, Andover. Fifty years later his classroom in stately Pearson Hall is still adorned with his posters. He also produced popular Latin comedies, complete with costumes and masks, coached hockey, and served on the board that set secondary school Latin examinations. We first lived in America House (where Samuel Smith had written "My Country 'tis of Thee") with fourteen boys, and later in Adams Hall where our son Michael was born in 1938. Diana, our daughter, followed in 1942 after we had moved to a house on Highland Road.

Brooks School in North Andover invited Bill to be head of the Classics Department, and we moved there in 1944. His library of classical texts now resides in a classroom there. Through his work on the Board of Latin Examiners he had met

John C. Jenkins, headmaster of St. Bernard's School in New York City. It came as a great surprise to us when Mr. Jenkins asked Bill if he would succeed him as headmaster. This was a tough decision; Bill was content in his work at Brooks and later said that St. Bernard's was the only school where he would have considered being headmaster. We moved to New York City in 1949 for what turned out to be twenty-two happy, demanding and rewarding years at St. Bernard's. An advantage to us over boarding-school life was our relationship with a wonderful group of parents who took us into their hearts and homes.

In these summers we were lucky to be able to travel to England, Canada, Australia and Italy, and to receive a Ford grant enabling us to spend six months visiting schools in England, Scotland, France and Belgium. Another great interest grew out of the request from a former St. Bernard's father, Mr. Jaeger, to help found a school in Puerto Rico. The Americans who worked at the sugar plantations in Fajardo found it too far to send their children to the American school in San Juan, and the local Catholic school did not offer an adequate curriculum to prepare students for American preparatory schools. A St. Bernard's Old Boy, William Dean, filled in nobly as a temporary head for six months until Bill found a most suitable couple, Ronald and Angela Lawson, to take over.

In 1940 we purchased a house in Chatham, Massachusetts, where the family enjoyed many wonderful summers until we became permanent residents following Bill's retirement from St. Bernard's in 1972 at the age of 67. After a few years of living like Horace on his Sabine farm, he became a lay reader at St. Christopher's Church, and was elected a member of the Chatham Public Schools Committee where he remained very active for twelve years until 1980. A Westgate Teachers' Fellowship Fund for the Chatham schools was founded in his memory.

Bill continued to have contented years as the proud father of Michael and Diana and grandfather of Ramsay, born 1973, and Katie, born a year later. Bill continued to garden until near the end. For his eightieth birthday he requested a pitch fork and still managed long rows of raspberries, four bee hives and many vegetables. He also experimented with hens, geese, sheep and goats with varying degrees of success. In May, 1987 he learned he had cancer, but had a happy last visit with his cousins in England that October. On July 27th, 1988 he died at home, alert and caring to the end.

— XV —
DOWN THE STAIRCASE,
& UP WITH SCHOOL

The following article was written by Bill at the request of Fessenden Wilder, Senior Master and Editor of The Archbishop, *a parent-alumni bulletin of Brooks School, North Andover, Mass., and published in the April, 1968 issue. At the time of writing, Bill was Head Master of St. Bernard's. Reprinted with permission of Brooks School.*

Must all new teachers now be professionally trained, fully authenticated, labelled MAT and paid by a union scale? The answer may be a guarded "Yes, provided the administrators are correspondingly reliable and discerning, and hardheaded about notions of tenure." A brave new world! if far removed from Galilee. Mr. Wilder thinks some readers may be interested in turning from this efficient program of tomorrow to the more haphazard training of yesterday, and asks me to write on the subject autobiographically. It is flattering to write for *The Archbishop* and thus build for oneself, if I may immodestly borrow from the immodest Horace, a monument more durable than bronze and loftier than the royal pile of the pyramids.

My one-track mind hardly considered any other profession than teaching, except keeping horses; and after relinquishing the rank of captain and adjutant in the First Hussars in the Canadian militia, I concentrated on teaching. For seven years I taught university students (the University of Western Ontario two years, Harvard and Radcliffe five years); for fourteen years in preparatory schools (Andover nine years, Brooks five); and now for eighteen years in an elementary school (St. Bernard's in New York City). After thus descending these steps of the system, I consider the lowest steps to be about the most interesting and important; for pupils live on these steps eight years—twice as long as they will in high school, or college, or graduate school; in fact will have spent almost all of their young lives here by the time they leave, and are of course much more impressionable and responsive at 6 to 14 than they will be again. The responsibilities of the elementary teacher correspondingly seem to me more vivid, more comprehensive, more grave, and more cheerful.

My first taste of teaching occurred in our parish Sunday school in Winnipeg at 16, along with a boyhood idol, Arnold Heeney, 18, later twice Ambassador to Washington, and then Canadian Chairman of the St. Lawrence International Seaway Commission. These Sunday afternoons taught me, and possibly my classes too, something about the Bible, which my father always read aloud to the family daily after breakfast, and also something of teaching techniques. My first paid teaching was done on a lonely Sioux Reserve in Manitoba, where about twenty Indian children, aged 4 to 16, straggled to my isolated hilltop house near the frame church at any hour after 5 a.m. and stayed till 3 p.m. My chief pastimes that summer were simple, reading through _Paradise Lost_, and shooting gophers from the bedroom window. The summer job paid my senior year's tuition in Manitoba University and reinforced a sense of pleasure in the company of children. It partly compensated for my loneliness.

A year of graduate studies in classics in Toronto actually proved more lonely. Graduates did not participate in undergraduate life and sports, and I had no teaching to do, no Sunday schoolers, no Sioux, no gophers. One aspect of teaching that attracts shy people is that they find companionship there as they may not find it elsewhere in society. This motive of easy friendship may not be admirable, but is usually harmless and may be creative. I have observed that school life occasionally develops quite feeble personalities into notable, even mighty, teachers. At least this motive is more agreeable than what animated Dionysius II of Syracuse: "Having been expelled by a revolution, he proceeded to open a school in Corinth, so insatiable was his lust to exercise power."

After three more years of classical studies at Oxford, where I perhaps unwisely avoided the School of Education, I was agreeably surprised to receive a two-year appointment as instructor in the University of Western Ontario, and as Dean of Residence in Huron Theological College where my father had studied and received an honorary Doctor of Divinity degree. The residence duties proved so enjoyable and absorbingly interesting that I declined to take the salary my first year, and also declined a post in Harvard as instructor, as I had signed up for two years in Canada. Both refusals turned out for the best, for Harvard repeated its offer a year later, in 1930, when I was more experienced; Huron doubled my second year's salary, and, by staying in London, Ontario, I met my wife. We were married five years later.

Boys and girls from Western Ontario and Michigan, largely rural, were sincere and appreciative if poorly trained students; the "theologs" were serious and in many cases senior to me; daily chapel was devout; and our small Classics Department of five men, hailing from Harvard, Oxford, Cambridge and St. Andrews, unvexed by notions of publishing or perishing, read widely and taught singleheartedly. We were expected on request to visit outlying Ontario high schools to judge debates and oratorical contests,—unpaid duties that were compensated by the appreciation shown by the schools and the knowledge one gained of various high schools and communities. In class or out, those two university years were pleasant. I also had the use of two horses.

Harvard was a contrast. Its intellectual scope, like its library, was immensely larger, but its atmosphere more anxious and hollow; certainly bigger, doubtfully better. One would have been daunted,—as was a countryman of mine who returned to Western Canada, indignant and dismayed in his first February, — but for at least five advantages: the interest of teaching some very able and well-trained and selected students at Harvard and Radcliffe (two men are now distinguished classics professors at great universities); the privileges of Widener Library; with its stacks wide open until 10 p.m.; many new friends, senior and contemporary; a huge selection of courses available; and easy access to a cluster of fine preparatory and high schools. I spent interesting hours or weekends, in my five Harvard years, at St. Mark's, Andover, Exeter, Deerfield, Middlesex, St. Paul's, St. George's, Portsmouth Priory, Milton, Boston Latin and Roxbury Latin. When the great Dr. Peabody had me spend two days and a night at Groton, I was surprised to encounter there my revered senior professor E.K. Rand sitting in Mr. DeVeau's II Form Latin class, wedged so firmly into a small boy's desk that dignity and the laws of gravity forbade his being eased out of it till all the class had left the room.

These visits confirmed in me a wish to begin my downward course into schools. Many boys of 15 or 16 were wasting time, I thought, in school, and could easily do "college work." The Classical Department gave me a free hand in 1932 to set advanced Latin papers and offer a prize, if I could find some money for the prize, so as to "stretch" able boys well beyond the scope of the College Entrance Latin exams. I offered for the prize part of my salary ($2,200.00 in 1932). When the chairman mercifully refused, I searched and found a certain George Emerson Lowell scholarship existed, paying about $500.00 to a boy who "excelled in Classics and Athletics." This scholarship, after some determined debating, was made available for my purpose, and still is. I gladly set and corrected all the Lowell Scholarship papers in Latin and Greek for the next three years that I stayed at Harvard (1933-35), and this put me in closer touch still with a dozen or more good schools. A happy sequel occurred in my first year at Brooks, 1944-45, when for the first time a Brooks boy, Richard Prescott, a pupil of Mr. Carr's and mine, won the George Emerson Lowell Prize. The bread cast upon the waters in 1932 had returned after many days — actually, after thirteen years.

The grim pursuit of the Ph.D. convinced me perhaps hastily to leave college, for it had cost too much in long nights of weary study lasting often till 3 a.m.; especially as this labor had to fit into full days of teaching at Harvard and Radcliffe. With periodic extra tasks thrown in, like grading a hundred exams in ancient authors for the Department of English and History, one had little time or spirit for the social or athletic life one had enjoyed in Oxford and Canada, surely important to healthy bachelors of 26 to 30. My graduate studies were enthusiastic under Professor E.K. Rand, on a congenial topic in the life of Charlemagne, but when Mr. Rand left for a year at the Sorbonne, I had to change my thesis from Charlemagne to a more philological and fretful topic of fidgety interest and little discernible value.

These grim months brought, of course, some gloomy profit. Thus, in comparison with those three-foot stacks of blue books written at top speed by college seniors, my present little Sixth Grade dictation papers or even the essays of Grade VIII now seem short, sweet and simple. Furthermore, the study of Greek and Latin philology in depth under the world's top man, Joshua Whatmough, has illuminated for a lifetime the historical development of the ancient languages, tracing and explaining their felicitous structures. For instance, I once thought the ablative case a bloated, monstrous feature of the Latin language, a hydra bulging with sprouts, knobs and warts labeled obscurely as "ablative absolute," "ablative of comparison," "ablative of place from " and the like,—sixteen of them for the bewildered student to memorize.

I learned to think differently. The ablative case was, I now found, more like a well trained elephant, cleverly carrying a vast load of meanings, venerable in its history, an ingenious and economical organ of Latin expression. When a new Latin schoolbook comes into my hand, I like to inspect its treatment of this reverend and veteran creation. If the author sees in it only a dozen or sixteen lesson topics and exercises to be stuffed somewhere into his book, I feel he is a journeyman, not a philologist; and though his book may cost a fancy price, with colored maps and pictures, it still seems to me pragmatic and pedantic, not scholarly. Pedantry on glossy paper I rate far below accurate scholarship, but the former now floods an expanding and therefore vulgarized market. How useful to remember the caustic epigram coined in Alexandria in wordy, windy times like ours: ἐγα βιβλιον, ἐγα κακόν "Big book? big nuisance."

Publishers nowadays make big money in peddling expensive and inflated school books. Can pupils trained, or shall I say gorged, on these ever have time, leisure or taste for scholarship, the life of "active leisure"? Won't they in turn become soft, restless and shallow teachers, never having had time to be touched by the sustaining intelligent power of unhurried wonder? Many schoolrooms are already manned by such, and it is too bad when school heads are slow or supine in discerning between them and studious teachers. The types are as distinguishable as the hireling is distinguishable from the good shepherd in St. John's Gospel, and school heads are not doing well for their children if they indulgently foster the feeble or counterfeit along with the searching and genuine. Herein lies the great danger to pupils in the difficult matter of "teacher tenure."

The younger the pupils, the greater the need of carefully selecting genuine persons to teach them, good shepherds, not hirelings. One may distinguish three periods or levels of formal schooling, and three teaching types appropriate to these levels. In the youngest or primary level, up to say Grade V or VI, a child forms his habits and attitudes largely by imitation and by almost uncritical obedience or absorption or adaptation. When a child is so vulnerable to all impressions, his trust being absolute and the impressions so durable, the best possible personalities are needed. Primary teachers need not know a great deal, but what they know and teach must be truthful, and their own emotional life must be truthful, sincere, warm and healthy.

In the oldest and last level, college students possess already independent and matured motives for seeking knowledge, and a professor who is learned and lucid may satisfy their desire even though he may be afflicted by many personal and emotional ills, for his private joys, fears, angers, anxieties and the like are of little account in the college transaction.

High school stands intermediate. Here the teacher must know his subject well or lively adolescents will excel him, yet he must also be something of a model of character, so that his students, still plastic in character themselves, will respect him as a visible symbol, and to some extent wish to resemble and follow him.

In France the primary teacher, working in Grades I—V, is called *instituteur*, as one who brings up children to take their places in the structures and institutes of civilized life. The other teachers, be they engaged in the *lycée* (for ages 11—18) or the university, are *professeurs*. Personally I am glad to have worked and felt at home at both levels, to have had twenty-one years as a *professeur* in Western Ontario, Harvard and Radcliffe, Phillips Andover and Brooks, and now to be spending nineteen years as *instituteur*, training young children, I hope truthfully, in truthful manners and truthful attitudes.

The most perfect, I think, of Virgil's poems is the one about country life and the small but epic world of bees. They have their customs and their laws, their strifes and loyalties and successes, and he who studies and serves them in their puny world can learn a lot and take pride in his work. A few words from the fourth Georgic of Virgil can end my pages and voice my feelings: *In tenui labor, at tenuis non gloria, si quem Numina laeva sinunt auditque vocatus Apollo.*

Small is the scope of my work, but not small the glory, if fortune assists me and God gives answers to my prayers.

— XVI —
REFLECTIONS BY HIS CHILDREN

MY FATHER

At 82 I know you've had more than your share of life
And we of you.
I try to prepare myself for
What the future must bring,
But there is no way to prepare for loss.
We may dread it, rationalize it, but when it comes,
Its pain will still be hard to bear.
When you are gone, the memories I now have
Could be just the same,
Except knowing there can be no more
Will shroud them with a grief that's absent now.

When I first heard of your heart attack,
I could only think such thoughts as these.
Seeing you in hospital next day,
Your mind full of the book you had just read
And how to help the election of a friend,
My sad thoughts disappeared,
And I marvelled once more at the man you are,
At the joy you take from life
To give it back in so many helpful ways.

I must not dwell on what we'll lose in you,
But rejoice in happy memories, as you would do.

—*Diana Westgate*
(May, 1987)

St. Christopher's Episcopal Church
Chatham, Massachusetts
August 9, 1988

We are gathered here today not to mourn the passing of my father, Bill Westgate, but to give thanks—thanks for the things he did while he was alive and thanks for the people he touched and who will carry on where he left off.

He spent his life educating himself and others. His love for the classics began early and continued to the end.

He immersed himself in everything he did. When Virgil extolled the virtues of beekeeping, he decided to try it. Driving two hives of bees from Andover to Chatham about 1947, he drove too fast over some railroad tracks, and the bee hives went flying. He was able to stop the car, escape with a few dozen stings, set things to rights, and keep on driving. He kept bees, producing about 100 pounds of honey annually until they died in 1987, a year before he did.

When Horace extolled the virtues of gardening, gardening became more than a hobby. His father's upbringing on a farm in Watford, Ontario, combined with his own study of the classics resulted in his naming our place on Cedar Street "Scholar Tree Farm." He never quite resigned himself to the fact that Horace had probably over 100 slaves and his grandfather had ten sons and a daughter. He had to make do with two children and two grandchildren.

When he retired from St. Bernard's School in 1971 he was able to combine his experience as a teacher and administrator while serving on the Chatham School Committee with gardening and playing his cello.

Beginning with his teaching in 1928 at the University of Western Ontario, then at Harvard and Radcliffe, Phillips Academy, Brooks School, St. Bernard's and finally in Chatham, where his last term ended in 1986, he taught or provided counsel for the teaching of several thousand students. Since he taught in reverse chronological order (from university to elementary school) his former students now range in age from 8 to 80.

When one of his first students at Harvard, Buz Gummere, came to dinner a year ago, he and Buz spent one third of dinner quoting Cicero to each other. Their conversation was largely in Latin. Here is a translation of two passages they both liked and remembered from Cicero's *De Senectute*. The quotes are those of Cato in 150 B.C., then 84 years old, holding an imaginary conversation with two younger men in their 30's:

So people who declare that there are no activities for old age are speaking beside the point. It is like saying that the pilot has nothing to do with sailing a ship because he leaves others to climb the masts and run along the gangways and work the pumps, while he himself sits quietly in the stern holding the rudder. He may not be doing what the younger men are doing, but his contribution is much more significant and valuable than theirs. Great deeds are not done by strength or speed or physique: they are the products of thought, and character, and judgement. And far from diminishing, such qualities actually increase with age.

(from the chapter on "Activities for the Old")

All things in keeping with nature must be classified as good; and nothing is so completely in keeping with nature than that the old should die. When the same fate some- times attacks the young, nature rebels and resists: the death of a young person reminds me of a flame extinguished by a deluge. But the death of the old is like a fire sinking and going out of its own accord, without external impulse. In the same way as apples while green can only be picked by force, but after ripening to maturity fall off by themselves, so death comes to the young with violence but to old people when the time is ripe.

(from the chapter entitled "Death Has No Sting")

Bill Westgate was active to the end, making telephone calls the day before he died. The last one he received was from his grandson Ramsay. His last day's mail included letters from his granddaughter Katie.

He also had a wonderful conversation with the Baker Brothers, who had just finished mowing the lawn about 4:00 p.m. They thanked him for having testified on their behalf at a public hearing. "It is a democracy," he replied. They persisted in thanking him. "Well, democracy only works if people are willing to fight for other people's rights," he said.

The night of July 26-27 was the first night when his family had to bring in an outside nurse. About 4:00 a.m. he decided the time was ripe for him. We cannot thank the Hospice nurses enough. With their help, even in death, Bill Westgate made life fuller—not emptier—for his family and friends.

We pray that he joins his many friends in the afterlife and that we here today continue to appreciate and pass on to others what he has taught us. He would have been touched, as we are touched, at how many of you have come to fill this church today.

—*Michael D.M. Westgate*

"He needs no epitaph to guard a name
Which man shall praise while worldly work is done.
He lived and died for good—be that his fame.
Let marble crumble. This is living stone."

—From Bill's diary, 1965
Source unknown

INDEX

Abbott-Smith, Dr., 170
Abbott-Smith, Mrs., 170
American Philological
    Association, 176
Americans at Balliol, 133,
    136, 150, 152–53
Astor, Lady, 130–31

Bailey, Charlie, 35–36
Bailey, Cyril, 50, 51, 65, 109,
    111, 112, 114, 115–16,
    119–20, 149–50, 151, 156,
    169
Balliol College, Oxford, 46,
    48–51, 65, 91, 93, 94, 99
    preparation for, 100
    Westgate at, 109, 110–22,
    123–34, 148, 149–60,
    161–75, 176
Balliol rowing, 110, 113–14,
    162–66, 176
Bell, Kenneth, 112
Biarritz, 105, 106, 119, 145
Blair, Andy, 17
Boat Club (Balliol), 110, 169
Bonnycastle family, 17, 18, 21,
    23
Bonnycastle, Humphrey
    66, 67, 74, 129, 130
Bonnycastle, Mrs., 78
Borough, Burton, 138–39, 140,
    141–42, 143

Borough, Cynthia, 142, 143,
    157
Borough, Lysette, 135–136,
    138, 141, 144, 157
Borough, Mrs., 135–37, 138,
    142–44, 157
Brasenose College, Oxford, 46,
    162–66, 171
Brett, Mr., 68, 70
British Museum, 62
Brooke, Rupert, 156–57
Brooks School, 10, 177–78,
    180, 183, 186
Buchanan, Will, 69
Burman, Walter, 16
Butlers (the), 167
Butler, Enid 159, 166, 167,
    168, 174, 175

Cambridge University, 167,
    176
Chatham (MA) Public Schools
    Committee, 178
Cheney, Sir John, 44
Church Missionary Society
    (CMS), 1, 4, 7, 10
Clarendon, Countess of,
    129–31, 147, 171, 172
Clarendon, Earl of, 129
Classical Association of New
    England, 176–77
Cosgrave, F.H., 97, 99

Crawford, Dr. Edmund
(Eddie), 1, 6, 52, 56, 58, 61
Crawford, Kathleen Malone,
1–2, 6, 48, 58, 61, 103,
131, 145, 150, 158
Crosthwait, Cameron, 88, 96
Crowe, Harold, 17–18, 19, 20

Dean, William, 178
De Pauley, Miss, 34
De Pauley, William, 17, 75
Drury, Lady, 110, 119, 121,
123, 132, 158, 166

Eccleshall Castle, 142–43
Edward the Black Prince, 53

France, 89, 91, 94, 98, 104–6,
144–47
French, Mrs., 135, 136, 138,
139

Gates (American student), 152
Geddes, Sir Auckland, 174,
175
Geddes, Ross, 159
Gee, Mr., 10–11, 34, 49
George Emerson Lowell
Scholarship, 183
Goff, Diana, 172
"Greats" (Oxford
examinations), 122, 174,
176
Griswold Women's Missionary
Society, 32–33
Grolier Society, The, 78
Groves, Helen, 159, 175

Hammond, Mason, 110, 133,
144, 145
"Handshaking", 116, 119–21,
156
Harvard University, 10, 176–
77, 180, 182–83, 186
Havard, Miss, 29, 30
Heeney, Arnold, 181
Hidden, Stanley, 104–5
Hodgins, Lloyd, 66, 77, 82
Honour Moderations ("Mods"),
98, 121–22, 124, 134, 158,
159, 162, 166, 168, 169
Westgate's reaction to
results of, 173–74, 175,
176
Hotán, Harry, 31
Huron Theological College, 1,
176, 182
Hutton, Maurice, 90, 169
Hyde Park, 59–60

Iffley Church, 112
Itoye, Jo, 25, 27

Jaeger, Mr., 178
Jebb, Dick, 140
Jenkins, John C., 178
Johnston, Wallace, 171
Jowett, Benjamin, 46

Keble College, Oxford, 34, 45–
46,
Kennaway, Sir John, 4, 5
Kershaw, Judge, 151–52
Kidd, Benjamin, 43, 45–46
Klaehn, John, 84–85
Knapton, Jack, 145

Lawson, Angela, 178

Lawson, Ronald, 178
Lear, Edward, 88
Lindsay, A. D., 111, 114
London, England, 62
Luckham, Dr., 150
MacDonald, James, 23, 24, 26, 27, 29
McDougall, Donald, 110, 112, 129–131, 144, 171
McKaig, Clem, 106, 131, 145
McKaig, Jim, 106, 107, 109, 131, 145, 148
MacKay, Louis Alexander, 109, 112, 114, 120, 122, 131, 145, 151
McKenzie, Sir James, 9
MacLennan, Dave, 77–78
MacNaughton, John, 72–73, 78, 82, 90
Malone, Albert, 8, 9
Malone, Alfred, 10
Malone, Anthony, 1
Malone, Arabella, 8
Malone, Edmund, 1
Malone family, 9
Mansur, Dave, 39, 74, 80–81, 85, 86, 101, 124
Martin, Chester, 46, 78
Missionary Society of the Canadian Church, 7, 13, 15
Montreal, Canada, 39–40, 86
Morrison, Christopher, 171
"Morrison Fours," 113, 115, 150–51
Murdock, Murray, 17

Neill, Milly, 20, 21
Nightingale family, 4, 5–6

Noel, John, 25, 31

Olaf, Crown Prince, of Norway, 110, 176
Oriel College, 46
Owen, Mr., 82
Oxford University, 51, 93, 167
colleges of, 122 note1
ice hockey team, 176

Peabody, Dr., 183
Pelham, Henry, 164–65
Pickard-Cambridge, A. W. ("Picker"), 99, 112, 116, 119–20, 131, 132, 133, 144, 168, 169
on Westgate, 134
Phillips Academy, Andover, 10, 177, 180, 186
Prescott, Richard, 183
Prince of Wales, 130–31

Radcliffe, 10, 180, 183, 186
Rand, E. K., 183, 184
Reade, John, 73, 75, 77, 81–82, 84, 85, 88, 94
Religion, 75–76, 85–86, 91–92
Rhodes Scholar, 65, 77–78
Rhodes Scholarships, 23, 51, 67, 69, 71
Rhodes Trust, 112, 176
Royal Belfast Academical Institute, 10–11

St. Bernard's School, 10, 178, 180
St. Hilda's, 70, 72, 76, 79, 80, 83, 84, 96

St. John's College School,
16–17
Salisbury Cathedral, 44–45
Sands, Miss, 119
Shepperson, 141
Shrewsbury, 139–40, 144
Sioux Indian Reserve, 23–33,
181
Smith, A. L., 46–47, 48–49
Squire Scholarship, 43, 46
Streeter, Canon, 149, 170
Sykes, Bill, 36, 38

Togger Week, 161, 162–66
Towneley Plays, 116–18
Trinity College, Toronto, 18
note1, 66, 67
Annual Athletic Dinner,
79–80
"Bishop's Candidate," 74–75
Dramatic Society, 89–90
"Valedictory," 95–97
Westgate at, 69–76, 77–97,
98–100, 109, 110

University of Manitoba, 34, 63
University of Western
Ontario, 1, 10, 176, 180,
182, 186
Upper Canada College School,
93

Walker (Englishman), 36, 42
Watson, Beatrice, 8, 9, 11, 12,
14, 41–42, 123, 145
Watson, Hubert, 43 note1, 45,
49, 94, 123, 145, 150
Watson, John, 8, 11, 43 note1,
45, 49, 123, 136, 150

Watson, Kathleen, 8, 43
note1, 45
Watson, Mona, 145, 150, 173
Watson family, 9
Westgate, Alan, 14
Westgate, Alec, 14, 66, 68, 69
Westgate, Anna, 14
Westgate, Diana, 177, 178,
187
Westgate, Dorothy, 3, 6–7, 31,
64, 93, 94, 105, 106, 138
childhood, 8, 9, 10, 13, 14
in England, 100, 110, 119,
158, 159, 172–73
trip to France, 144–45
Westgate, Henrietta Georgina
Humphrey Malone (Rita),
1–2, 3–4, 11–12, 63, 72,
108, 170, 174
in Ireland, 7–9, 10
move to Canada, 13, 14
trip to England, 100, 105,
110, 114
Westgate, Margaret, 14
Westgate, Maureen (Moll),
2–4, 7, 25, 26, 31, 63, 67,
70, 93, 94–95, 132, 145,
154
childhood, 6, 8, 9, 10, 13, 14
trip to England, 100, 105,
110, 114, 115
Westgate, Michael, 177, 178
Westgate, Minnie, 14
Westgate, Palmer, 2, 14
Westgate, Ralph, 14
Westgate, Reginald Isaac
Wilfred (Bill)
childhood, 1, 2, 4, 5–15
education, 7, 10–11, 12, 15,

16–17, 34, 63, 181–82
—Balliol, 109, 110–22,
123–34, 148, 149–60,
161–75, 176
—evaluation of
achievement, 156, 173–74
—Greek and Latin studies,
15, 16, 34, 90, 91, 94, 98,
112, 114, 115–16, 119–21,
132, 161–62, 168
—reading, 10, 24, 30–31, 55,
65, 87, 91, 92, 121, 123,
139, 156, 161–62, 175
—Trinity College, Toronto,
69–76, 77–97, 98–100,
109, 110
personal characteristics, 7,
10
summer jobs, 16–33
on teaching, 180–86
teaching career, 10, 176–79,
180–85, 186
Westgate Teachers Fellowship
Fund, 178
Westgate, Thomas Buchanan
Reginald (Rex), 182
advice to son, 100–101
in Canada, 14–15, 16, 17,
21, 23, 32, 34, 63, 68–69,
71, 75, 94, 170, 177
Canadian roots, 13–15
missionary work, 1–3, 7, 10,
11–12
Westgate, Will, 14
Westminster Abbey, 60
Whatmough, Joshua, 184
Whitgift Grammar School, 7,
9, 10, 57–58
Wilder, Fessenden, 180

Wilson, Roy, 151–52, 154–56
Wood, Freddy, 153, 166,
172–73
World War I, 7–9, 11–12
Wright, B. J. F., 169
Wycliffe, John, 46
Young, Norman, 34